HISTORY AND STORY OF 'A' BATTERY
84TH ARMY BRIGADE R.F.A.
(Late 262nd Battery, R.F.A.)

I have made for you a song,
And it may be right or wrong,
But only you can tell me if it's true;
I have tried for to explain,
Both your pleasure and your pain,
And, Thomas, here's my best respects to you.

Rudyard Kipling.

The History

OF

'A' Battery
84th Army Brigade

ROYAL FIELD ARTILLERY

1914 – 1919

D. F. GRANT, M.C.
(LATE MAJOR R.F.A.)

The Naval & Military Press Ltd

published in association with

FIREPOWER
The Royal Artillery Museum
Woolwich

Published by
The Naval & Military Press Ltd
Unit 10 Ridgewood Industrial Park,
Uckfield, East Sussex,
TN22 5QE England
Tel: +44 (0) 1825 749494
Fax: +44 (0) 1825 765701
www.naval-military-press.com

in association with

FIREPOWER
The Royal Artillery Museum, Woolwich
www.firepower.org.uk

The Naval & Military Press

MILITARY HISTORY AT YOUR FINGERTIPS

... a unique and expanding series of reference works

Working in collaboration with the foremost regiments and institutions, as well as acknowledged experts in their field, N&MP have assembled a formidable array of titles including technologically advanced CD-ROMs and facsimile reprints of impossible-to-find rarities.

In reprinting in facsimile from the original, any imperfections are inevitably reproduced and the quality may fall short of modern type and cartographic standards.

Printed and bound by Antony Rowe Ltd, Eastbourne

DEDICATION

To my gallant comrades in "A" Battery, 84th Army Brigade R.F.A.—officers, N.C.O.'s and men, alas, many, too many, of them fallen, but who never will be forgotten—with whom it was my good fortune and pride to be so long and closely associated in the anxious and strenuous days of the Great War, 1914-1919.

"We shall not pass this way again"

D. F. G.

February, 1922.

CONTENTS

CHAPTER I.

Formation of the Battery.—Improvised Equipment.—Original Officers. — Christmas, 1914. — Warren Heath, Ipswich.—March to Salisbury Plain.—Inspection by H.M. the King 13

CHAPTER II.

Arrival in France.—In Action near Meaulte.—Visit of H.M. the King and President Poincaré.—Bdr. J. C. Steptoe 24

CHAPTER III.

Christmas, 1915.—" Tests " 29

CHAPTER IV.

Fricourt.—Suzanne.—Sports at Argoeuves.—Billon Wood.—Lieut. E. N. Dexter leaves 32

CHAPTER V.

Battle of Somme, July 1st, 1916.—Creeping Barrage, Introduction of.—Supporting 7th Queens.—Advance to Breslau Point.—Death of Lieut.-Col. D. Blois, D.S.O.—Caterpillar Valley.—Armentieres.—Thiepval.—Pozieres.—Blighty Wood.—Reorganisation as Six-gun Battery.—Christmas, 1916.—Tptr. Olney.—Calibration.—German Retreat.—West Miraumont Road.—Irles 36

CHAPTER VI.

84th Bde. becomes an Army Brigade.—Battle of Vimy Ridge.—Lieut. Platts wounded.—The Tunnel Position.—Willerval.—Battle for Oppy.—Sgt. Porter and Bdr. Hookway, Gallant Rescue by.—Battle of Messines Ridge.—Zillebeke Lake Position.—In

Rest at Houtkerque. — Poperinghe. — Flanders
Offensive, July 31st, 1917, Position for.—H.R.H.
the Prince of Wales visits A/84.—Night Firing.—
Advance to Pilchem Ridge.—Bdr. A. F. Bethell,
M.M., killed.—Short Rest.—Admirals Cross Roads
Position.—Advance to St. Julien.—Shooting by
Map.—Spot Farm.—Gallantry of Bdr. A. J. Pick-
wick.—Christmas, 1917   50

CHAPTER VII.

In Action near Festubert.—German Offensive, March,
1918.—Gunner W. Nutter killed.—Splendid work
by Lieut. Darley and Corp. Allum.—Lys Retreat.—
St. Venant.—" Scrounging."—In Rest at Le Vielfort. — Sports. — In Action near Loos. — " Returns."—Annequin.—Preparations for Open Warfare.—Assault on Hindenburg Line.—Position in
Le Cateau.—Forêt de Mormal, Battery's last Position.—Withdrawal to Maretz.—The Armistice   ...   73

CHAPTER VIII.

H.M. the King visits Maretz.—Race Meetings.—
Christmas, 1918.—Demobilisation starts.—Move to
Bertry.—Down to Cadre Strength.—Disbandment
at Dover.   85

APPENDIX :—Awards.—Things We Should Like to
Know.—Abbreviations.—Index.—List of Officers.

FOREWORD

BY

LIEUT.-GENERAL SIR IVOR MAXSE, K.C.B.,
C.V.O., D.S.O.

Commanding 18th Division and XVIII Army Corps
1914-18.

IT gives me great pleasure to avail myself of Major Grant's invitation to write a foreword to his excellent little book, because I believe that this record of the services of a single battery of artillery will be valued by numbers of officers who did not serve in it. It will certainly be indispensable to all ranks who did.

We are inundated by books on the War; many of them deal with political or racial issues, are written by men with an axe of their own to grind, or are in fact a medium of propaganda to emphasise some doctrine or some grievance. Others are written by men who really believe that the war was won by politicians and in spite of the soldiers ; or by some civilian strategist who had never been under fire ; or by speeches made in 1914 or subsequently. Now the charm of this little book is that it is written for comrades who served together and are therefore acquainted with the episodes which the author narrates ; he is thus precluded from drawing upon a fertile imagination when his diary happens to be deficient in dramatic incident.

Indeed " A " Battery, 84th Brigade, R.F.A., 18th Division, whose story is here briefly chronicled,

was fortunate in one respect and may even be unique.
From its enrolment in October, 1914, when 300
patriots confronted their youthful officer—himself
on parade for the first time in that capacity—until
its demobilisation in May, 1919, " A " Battery had
but one Commander, and he is the author of this
book. His was the privilege, shared by scarcely any
other Commander, of leading into battle between
1914 and 1918 the unit of troops which he had himself created, of wielding the weapon he had forged
with his own hand. I am sure he will agree with me
that his was an unforgettable experience, but I also
hope he has not jumped to the erroneous conclusion
that his untrained battery of patriots was as useful
in 1914 as was a battery of Germans which had then
been in training for 20 consecutive years ?

I ask the question humbly, because some of the
gentlemen who think they won the war appear also
to think that military training is unnecessary ; or
that no wars will be waged in future ; or that the
League of Nations will take the place of armed
forces.

At any rate, the men of Great Britain who
answered Lord Kitchener's call in September and
October, 1914, represented the cream of our nation,
judged by any standard. In later days heavy sacri-
fices were made, and all, whether conscript or volun-
teer, fought with gallantry and determination. As
soldiers, hating war, they meant to see the thing
through, and they did. But it is true to say that
the recruts of 1914 joined up in a spirit of patriotism
and knightly adventure. Their ideals were great
and their difficulties even greater. I shall never forget the immensity of the task which confronted us
when I returned from the Mons Retreat and the
Battles of the Aisne to command the 18th Division

at Colchester, and helped to create its Artillery—a technical arm requiring skill and practice in the use of mechanical instruments, all of which were unobtainable, and some of which were only " made in Germany " !

Those of us who, like Major Grant, laboured to put into a few months the work of many years, can realise how heavily the nation paid in blood and hard cash for our flat refusal to face obvious facts and prepare for a war with Germany. The task was accomplished and the war ultimately won, but it took four years instead of one, and success was due to the tireless spirit, courage and cheerfulness with which the officers and men of " A " Battery and hundreds of thousands of others tackled their job throughout four hideous years of " unexpected " war. It is due to the whole of the Artillery of the 18th Division to say that its *esprit de corps* and its training were fully equal to that of its infantry.

To indicate what it means in flesh and blood to prolong a war, it may be stated that no less than 35 officers and some 600 other ranks passed through this single battery of six guns in the $4\frac{1}{2}$ years of its existence. Having fought in all the Battles of the 18th Division in 1915, 1916 and till March, 1917, this battery became an " Army " Battery and took part in the Battles of Vimy Ridge, Messines, Flanders, 1917, the Retreat of March, 1918, and the counter offensive of August, 1918. It served throughout its strenuous existence in France in all the five British Armies, and was for varying periods of time in fifteen different Army Corps and under thirty-five Divisional Commanders. The mere recital of so many changes of master is typical of what was occurring in most Brigades of British Artillery and is only mentioned as it illustrates one weakness of our improvised military forces, created after the outbreak of a war. I do not think that either the French or German batteries were so constantly shifted or so continuously in action over such long periods of consecutive fighting as were the British. We had started with a heavy handicap as ENGLAND the UNPREPARED. Everything had to be improvised as we slowly increased the number of our civilian soldiers. The strain put upon our artillery in France was stupendous. The one thing which saved them a little in 1915 and 1916 was the fact that ammunition was woefully lacking. Instead, we had in England several speeches on ammunition supply, but our gunners could not let them off on the enemy!

In conclusion, I congratulate Major Grant, M.C., on his record of service and on the story he has told of his beloved battery, but would entreat him to believe that Staff Officers on active service have objects in life beyond the exhibition of smart clothes and the creation of unnecessary difficulties for subordinate commanders.

IVOR MAXSE.

York, April, 1922.

CHAPTER I.

GATHERED together, from various recruiting offices, at the Suffolk Regiment's barracks at Bury St. Edmunds, were some 500 of all sorts and conditions of men who had answered Lord Kitchener's call during September and the first half of October, 1914. While they were collecting here a dozen stalwart Metropolitan police constables tried to teach them how to march, and left and right turn. There were no military instructors at all. Here also most of them submitted to the doctor's knife and were vaccinated. To digress for a moment. It was discovered afterwards that this doctor was a Hun, and that may explain why so many suffered with septic arms, and one poor fellow died.

On the morning of 17th October, 1914, they were all paraded and handed over to a young subaltern of the R.F.A. Poor fellow, this was his first parade as an officer, and so his feelings when he saw these 500 men in civilian clothes drawn up in front of him were indescribable. With the help of four of the afore-mentioned P.C.'s, he marched them to the station, entrained for Colchester, and eventually arrived at Colchester Artillery Barracks. The 18th Divisional Artillery was being formed here. The young sub. was overjoyed to find, on counting, that none of his flock had been lost, stolen or strayed since leaving Bury St. Edmunds.

The party was split up into groups of 100 each, 300 forming "C" Brigade, and the remaining 200

"D" Brigade (the next day the numbers 84 and 85 were allotted instead of the letters C and D). And so the first 100 came to be 262nd Battery R.F.A., the name being changed in January, 1915, to "A" Battery, 84th Brigade, R.F.A., on the formation of a fourth battery in the Brigade. The poor young subaltern, who will by now possibly be recognised as the writer, was told to make a battery of them, and was shown a pile of 21 tents to do it with! After considerable worrying round, some rations were found, but nowhere to cook and no one to cook. However, two volunteers offered to do their best in this respect. It is interesting to note that one of these good fellows, Corp. R. Venneear, remained as cook till 1918, when he took over the running of the battery canteen. When one thinks of those early days, till the 'Q' Dept. got properly going, one is convinced that they were as bad, or almost, in the matter of food, as the battery ever went through.

It was only that unquenchable spirit and that unexampled keenness of everyone to become a soldier that overcame these and all other difficulties and enabled us to carry on. It was this same spirit that pulled us through in the matter of training for the first six months. No uniforms came till the end of November, and even then they were those appalling blue affairs, nicknamed convicts' dress. It was not until just before Christmas, 1914, that khaki began to come in. In the same way we had to improvise and use makeshifts in the matter of equipment—wooden guns, dial sights, and directors. If the " gun " was loaded smartly the wooden shell was sent several feet from the muzzle of the " gun " by the impetus given to it by the

No. 4! We also began to learn field movements on the Abbey Fields. Six men, marching in half sections, with a red flag, represented a gun team, and six men with a white flag pretended to be a wagon team. On these fields also we twisted and contorted our bodies before breakfast in Swedish drill.

Our first eleven horses arrived on 11th November, 1914. On these and later arrivals, and with saddles lent under Lord Roberts' efforts, our rookies began to learn to ride.

The battery was now being made up to strength (134) with drafts from the Brighton Reserve Brigade —all splendid fellows—and other depôts. Of officers there joined on formation, 2nd Lieuts. E. N. Dexter, F. J. Rice (afterwards major of C/82 Bgde. R.F.A.), and H. J. Griffin (afterwards a major R.F.A.), and as officer commanding 2nd Lieut. D. F. Grant.

After a short time twelve old rifles were issued to us, but it might have been dangerous to have fired them. Still, they served for drill purposes, and gave us the idea that we could fight if need be. However, we had secret orders that if a German landing did occur we were to march inland. Secret instructions were even issued as to which civilian vehicles and horses were to be requisitioned to carry our kits. But the navy kept " Jerry " at home.

Our first Christmas approached. In August many of us thought, and were even afraid, that the war would have been over by now; and so those who did not get leave to celebrate Christmas at their own homes decided to make it as joyous a time as possible. The battery, fortunately, obtained permission to use the Parish Room of the local church.

For days beforehand the indefatigable B.Q.M.S. R. J. Bewell was making arrangements for decorations and provender, and when the day arrived the battery thoroughly appreciated the result of his efforts. Friends of the battery had subscribed sufficient for us to augment the rations considerably, and with the help of Venneear and his assistants a very enjoyable and hearty meal was spread, helped on its way with several barrels of beer. A cheery singsong was afterwards held by those still capable, and applause from those who were not! The battery was now housed in billets in private houses close to the Barracks, and these householders individually entertained in the evening those billeted on them. And so ended a very happy Christmas.

On 13th February, 1915, a motley crowd marched to Warren Heath Camp, near Ipswich. We had two very old pattern French 7.5 cm. guns (rumour had it that they were used at the Battle of Hastings!). We also had a "bucksheesh" G.S. wagon. This wagon was the beginning of our "extra," or unofficial transport, in the denial of the possession of which it is feared more official lies have been told by O.C.'s than anything else—always excepting the famous " destroyed by enemy shell-fire" saving clause.

The huts at Warren Heath were only in course of erection, and we left them, on 3rd May, 1915, before they were completely finished! However, our stay at Warren Heath was the happiest time of our nine months training in England. Horses and harness began to pour in, and, greatest of all, real 18 pounders arrived. Soon we were able to have mounted parades and field days, with three 18-pounders, and a water cart to represent the fourth gun (we were organised as a four-gun battery).

Colonel C. E. English had taken over the command of the Brigade shortly before it came to Warren Heath from Lt.-Colonel Dewar, who left us to join the 12th Division. This latter officer, who was dearly liked, we afterwards met as Area Commandant at Watou, in Belgium, in 1917. It was Col. English's ambition to be able to take the Brigade out at a trot along the roads at 8 miles per hour, and have no horse turn a hair. And it says much for the way the batteries trained and looked after their horses that in the end this was accomplished. Martlesham Heath was the scene of our mounted labours. Here we learnt " Sections, Right Wheel," " Halt, Action Front," and the more unofficial " Get those limbers away quicker," " Come along, you would have been able to have got a round off if you hadn't been such a long time unhooking that wagon," and so on. And a strange attraction that pretty heath had too, for after a hard morning's training there many fellows would go for a walk there in the evening with—not their own sisters !

It was at Warren Heath that we got that famous mule, Sammy, of evil memory. He would not be led to water on any account, he'd rather kick the camp down, but let him go unattended, and he would go like a lamb, and come back quietly to his stall when finished. It was impossible to put him into any vehicle, and so we eventually exchanged him with another unit in the 16th Division. It was his fine size that took their fancy; we didn't tell them of his character !

It was at Warren Heath also that the Brigade Ammunition Column was formed under Captain Constable, and to start which A/84 supplied its quota of personnel. Capt. Constable often used to say

B

afterwards that his best men and N.C.O.'s came
from "A" Battery.

On 3rd May, 1915, after a very happy three
months at Warren Heath, we marched out on our
way to Salisbury Plain. "A" Battery had already
gained a reputation for " spit and polish," and were
complimented by the major-general and our colonel
for our smart turn-out. Throughout the battery's
existence we always, of course, thought we were the
best battery in the brigade, and tried to show the
world this by our worship of the fetish " spit and
polish," and the condition of our horses.

On the first day's trek we marched back to our
old barracks at Colchester, where a rather amusing
incident happened on arrival. When we marched in
an A.S.C. corporal pointed out a pile of hay, and
said the rations would be along soon. "A" was the
leading battery of the brigade, and naturally
thought (?) that all the hay pointed out was for it.
In order to make no mistake about it, the hay was
ordered to be given the horses at once. It turned
out afterwards that the hay was intended for the
whole brigade, and in the mess later the other unit
commanders were heard complaining of the small
quantity of hay issued for their commands! He was
a smart boy that A/B.Q.M.S., and took full advantage of the battery arriving half-an-hour ahead
of the others. Captain Constable's column was the
chief sufferer, and to this day he chips the old
O.C. of A/84 with knowing something about, if not
instigating, the wangle!

The marching into Colchester Barracks on the 3rd
of May, 1915, marked a big corner in our history.
On 13th February we marched out of those gates
a mob with two ancient guns and a G.S. wagon;
while that day, only three short months after-

wards, we marched in complete with four guns, real 18 pounders, eight ammunition wagons, and nearly our full complement of horses and stores. It was indeed a proud day for us all. The afternoon was spent in polishing up for the next day's march, and the evening, some will remember, in saying " good-bye " to friends in our former billets in Colchester.

The next day (4th May, 1915), we marched to Braintree, and from there to Bishop's Stortford on the next day, arriving at Hertford on 7th May, 1915. There, two days later, 9th May, we entrained for Codford St. Mary, on Salisbury Plain. It was the first time many had entrained animals, and horses, mules (particularly the latter) and men learnt a lot !

Arrived at Codford St. Mary we marched to Heytesbury. Here, as at Warren Heath, we went into an unfinished hutment camp. For the next month we trained assiduously for practice camp. Bombardier A. F. Bethell worked hard at his signallers, and must often have dreamt at night that he was wagging " All guns 2 degs. more right," and for ever asking, " What's the delay?"

B.S.M. F. H. Turner, D.C.M., joined us on 25th June, 1915. This is a suitable place to put on record how much the battery owed to his untiring energy and constant desire to make it the best in the army. No O.C. could have had a more loyal and conscientious helper, whether it was in arranging the detail for a move on the following day, or in efficiently running a wagon line which the O.C. might not be able to see for weeks. There are a thousand and one ways in which a B.S.M. can hinder or help his O.C., and it can be honestly and sincerely recorded that B.S.M. Turner was out every time, and all the time, to help his officers, and particularly his O.C., whilst never forgetting his N.C.O.'s and men; all looked to him as their friend and helper. He was with us till August, 1918, when he went home to a Cadet School, having been strongly recommended for a commission " for services rendered in the field." He, like all Turners in the army, was nick-named " Twisty."

In the middle of June, 1915, we went to Hamilton Camp, near Lark Hill, for practice camp. There were many heartburnings and cold feet amongst all ranks at the prospect of generals and " brass hats " criticising their efforts at shooting. However, no bad mistakes were made, and the drivers, in par-ticular, did their work splendidly, and knew their drill movements to an inch; whilst those hard-hearted persons, the School of Gunnery staff, the directors of the Camp, were not stinting in their praise of the gunners and fire control.

After ten days we marched back to Heytesbury, and began to get ready for overseas. There were all sorts of rumours as to the theatre of war to which we were going—India and Egypt were the most men-tioned, till someone started the hare that someone else had been to the War Office, and whilst waiting in a room to interview an official had seen there a map of Italy with " 18th Division " pencilled on an area !

On 12th July, 1915, we had a great day. The battery was, with the rest of the 18th Division, in-pected by H.M. the King. For several days before we had been polishing up, and early on 12th July we marched to a spot between Fargo and Stonehenge and took up our position on the Divisional parade. An honour fell to the battery in providing the King's trumpeter, A. P. Olney, 1st Trumpeter of A/84, was chosen from all the trumpeters of the Division

as being the smartest turned out and best of the
badjis. The King, mounted on that beautiful black
charger of his, followed by Olney, first inspected us
drawn up in line at half interval. We then trotted
past the Saluting Base. His Majesty issued afterwards the usual complimentary order. This was
only the first of many such orders the 18th Division
received. At the Armistice the battery file was full
of them. They were, however, some acknowledg-
ment of the splendid training given the whole
Division by its major-general, Lt.-General Sir Ivor
Maxse, K.C.B., C.V.O., D.S.O., as he now is,
and who is rightly regarded as one of the finest
if not the finest, trainers of men that the nation has.
Towards the end of the war, after commanding the
18th Corps for some time, General Maxse was ap-
pointed Inspector General of Training. The 18th
Division became one of the crack divisions in the
B.E.F., and this was due in no small measure to the
training and leading it received from General
Maxse. This opinion is amply borne out by Capt.
G. H. F. Nichols (" Quex ") in his book " The
18th Division in the Great War "—a most enter-
taining and valuable work.

General Maxse was once inspecting battery positions near Meaulte in September, 1915, and finished
up his tour with A/84. The gunners and section
commanders fell in behind their gun pits, and after
General Maxse had very carefully inspected them he
turned round and said to Col. English and the O.C.,
" Ah, *these* men look like soldiers ; they're d——d
smart fellows." Apparently some previous units he
had seen had not pleased him.

The Divisional Artillery also had some very dis-
tinguished C.R.A.'s. The original C.R.A.,
Brigadier-General F. G. Stone, C.M.G., was suc-

ceeded in November, 1915, by Brigadier-General C.
van Straubenzee, C.B., C.M.G., who afterwards be-
came a major-general and G.O.C. R.A. Fifth Army.
He was succeeded in June, 1916, by Lt.-Col. S.
Metcalfe, C.M.G., D.S.O., commanding the 83rd
Brigade R.F.A., who was C.R.A. till he became
G.O.C. R.A. XI. Corps, after the 84th Brigade had
left the Division. When we returned to the 18th
Division in October, 1918, Lt.-Col. T. Seagram,
D.S.O., was the B.G. Thus we had the distinct
advantage of having great gunnery experts to com-
mand us.

The battery had only been in existence nine
months, and the high state of efficiency both as a
fighting and a spectacular unit it had attained was
truly marvellous. This was due, as has been stated
at the beginning, to the earnest desire of everyone
to become a soldier, and to " play the game." This
achievement of "playing the game" was the
greatest and strongest of the battery's foundations,
and the very small amount of crime and serious
offences committed by those who had been any length
of time in the battery showed the public opinion
and esprit de corps of A/84. This small amount
of crime caused Colonel English to remark
when he once had a prisoner from the battery
brought before him, " What! a prisoner from "A"
battery for me! " After all, any unit can be run
with crime and punishment, but it has to be a good
unit and have good fellows in it to carry on without.

During July, 1915, last leaves were given, and the
battery was got ready for overseas. Lt. Rice and
B.Q.M.S. Lewer were hard at work drawing final
stores and equipment, and in packing the vehicles
with the multitude of articles enumerated in A.F.
G. 1098. Poor Lewer was afterwards killed by a

shell entering his billet at Bethune, whilst he was asleep. Our first B.Q.M.S., R. J. Bewell, left us at Heytesbury to take a well deserved commission. Later on we met him in France as a captain and adjutant—at Meaulte and St. Julien.

Finally, at an early hour, on 26th July, 1915, we entrained for the last time in England, and detrained at Southampton, and it was apparently certain that we were at last en route for where we all wanted to go—France.

The following were the officers and senior N.C.O.'s who went across with the battery:—Captain D. F. Grant, Lt. F. J. Rice, Lt. E. N. Dexter, 2nd Lt. R. Darley, and 2nd Lt. W. T. Boston.

B.S.M. Turner, B.Q.M.S. A. Lewer, Sergt. W. Last, Sergt. A. Middleton ("A" sub.), Sergt. T. A. Shaw (" B " sub.), Sergt. J. J. Jones (" C " sub.), Sergt. J. Fleming (" D " sub.), and Farrier Sergt. A. Vincent.

CHAPTER II.

WE arrived at Havre early on the morning of the
27th July, 1915, disembarked, and after drawing a
few stores from the A.O.D., marched through the
town to a rest camp just outside.   The next morning
we entrained, and after a dreary and weary journey
in the train arrived at Longpré (near Amiens) late
at night, and marched to the village of Coisy. Here
most of us made our first acquaintance with " La
Belle France."   The first issue of pay in the new
active service pay books was made here.   Here also
we received our first strafing (from General Maxse,
by the way), for tying the picketing lines to fruit
trees in an orchard !   On 2nd August, 1915, we left
to " go into the line."   Many expected to gallop
into action, and take on a battalion of Huns advancing in close formation at the goose-step, in
proper Prussian (story book) style.   The reality was
distinctly flat in comparison.   We were to relieve
the French on the Somme, on the British line being
extended.   A couple of days before this an advance
party went up and had a look at the positions and
wagon lines.   With the French only one officer remained at the gun line during the night for the whole
brigade, the remainder retiring to comfortable billets
in Meaulte.   It didn't seem like war at all.   The
French officers told us the Huns would never fire
unless we did, and it was, in fact, " une très bonne
guerre."

The guns of the battery were taken up on the evening of the 3rd August. Strict orders were given that no smoking was to take place, and no shouting. Our breath was rather taken away when we arrived silently on the position by being welcomed with much shouting and cheers, and with many lanterns being waved by the French gunners of the 28th Brigade.

On 4th August, 1915, the guns were registered, and we formally took over the defence of the zone in front of Fricourt. Great was our delight at firing our first shells in action.

The wagon line was first situated at Meaulte on the River Ancre, some 15 miles N.E. of Amiens. Subsequently it was moved to Ville sur Ancre, 2½ miles nearer Amiens, after having been at Dernancourt for a short time. The guns, however, remained in the same position for over six months. Thus here we were able to specialise in " spit and polish," and " eyewash and whitewash " (both very much the same thing!). We only used to fire from 20 to 25 rounds a week, according to our restricted allowance. " The shell shortage " was an actual fact in France, whatever it may have been with the politicians. However, the small amount of ammunition used called for very little work on the part of the wagon line personnel; consequently their energies whilst at Ville sur Ancre were chiefly centred in making their quarters there perfect in every way. Stables were built, solid brick standings put down, billets improved, beds of wire netting constructed for all, model cook houses, ablution room, and dining hall erected. When all this had been accomplished Lt. Rice suggested that the tyres of the wagons should be burnished! But the idea got no further than repainting the vehicles.

One hundred rounds per gun were kept at the battery position, carefully cleaned and counted each day! The first four rounds of H.E. arrived in October, 1915. We fired one to see its action, etc., and as a consequence a written report was called for to explain why the O.C. had dared to fire one, " as the supply is so very limited." It was not until June, 1916, that the *Daily Mail*, or was it someone else? got the army anything approaching a sufficiency.

The battery took a small subsidiary part in the Battle of Loos in September, 1915, being given 150 rounds " to make a demonstration " at wire cutting. Battery commanders attended a lot of secret conferences, for practically nothing was allowed to appear on paper, as to our movements when we broke through! Vehicles were packed, and all got ready for the victorious march to Berlin. Alas! that it ended as it did.

[Note.—The present writer was on the Loos front when we eventually did break through—or the Germans retired—in October, 1918, and it was most interesting and instructive talking to the French civilians in towns and villages, such as Carvin, close behind the then front line. They and the Germans fully expected us to come through in 1915, and said that the current official German view was that had our attack been persisted in for another hour or so, the Germans would have given way.]

On October 27th, 1915, H.M. the King and President Poincaré visited the British Front, and passed through Mericourt, near to which village our wagon line was. It was a bitterly cold day, and it is feared that the biting wind rather nipped the loyal enthusiasm and delight of those who went to see the King go through, from the Divisional Commander downwards. This is easily understood, as the King was two hours behind scheduled time.

In November, 1915, Brigadier-General F. G. Stone (the C.R.A. 18th Division) and Col. C. E. English were posted to England, and were succeeded by Brigadier-General C. van Straubenzee and Lt.-Col. D. G. Blois.

The greatest interest was taken by the officer on duty at the O.P. in sniping at the enemy whenever he showed himself. The four guns of the battery were carefully laid on four selected and registered spots where observation had told that Germans were in the habit of appearing. On receipt of the order from the O.P., " Fire No. 2," for example, the lever would be pulled, and one of our scanty allowance would be speeding on its way to make Private Schmidt hurry along the road by Round Wood, above Fricourt. Bombardier J. C. Steptoe was the battery's very efficient look-out man, and he can lay claim to being the means of " bagging " a good many Germans in Bunny Wood and on the road at Target E. Steptoe would sit for hours with his eye glued to the telescope on a particular spot he suspected. The Divisional Intelligence Report ("Comic Cuts ") frequently contained items of his observation. In addition to being a very good look-out wallah, he was a splendid footballer; his footwork in particular being a pleasure to watch. He was

one of the bravest in action, and received a nasty
wound at the Battle of Vimy Ridge in April, 1917,
which got him to "Blighty." He rejoined us in
the autumn. He was the friend of all.

During this period 2nd Lieut. J. P. Phillips, who
was afterwards very badly wounded, and 2nd
Lieut. C. P. Lait joined the battery, and helped us
to "carry on" and keep cheerful.

CHAPTER III.

CHRISTMAS DAY, 1915, arrived with the battery still in action at Meaulte and the wagon line at Ville sur Ancre. On the morning of 25th December, the battery sent some eighty presents (weighing about eighteen pounds each) to our *vis à vis* on the other side of the front line. These Christmas presents were sent to spots in the enemy country where cooking or fires had been observed! The eighty rounds had been carefully saved up (quite unofficially) from our meagre weekly allowance, and for weeks previously this had necessitated sending in " cooked " returns of ammunition in possession.

One or two visits to Amiens and to neighbouring villages resulted in plenty of good food and liquor being provided for the Christmas dinners, supplemented by the very welcome parcels we had the pleasure of receiving from kind friends at home. " A " and " C " batteries officers' messes at the gun line combined for dinner that day, and enjoyed roast turkey and plum pudding; better could not have been served at the Piccadilly, or, at least, so it seemed to the diners. One can well imagine that the German " Comic Cuts " chronicled the information that " shouting and singing, and signs of great hilarity were heard behind the British lines during the evening of 25th December at Fricourt."

It is interesting to note here that the two remaining Christmas Days of the war were spent out in rest.

A battery is never without something to worry it, and one of these worries was " Tests." These tests were probably the result of a brain (?) wave of some brass-hat, and they were worked thus :

The battalion or the company commander of the unit the battery was covering would casually walk up to the telephonist of the attached artillery liaison officer and say : " Test Berlin." The telephonist would then ring up the battery and repeat the order. A round would then be fired on the enemy trench called Berlin. The time would be taken, by the infantry, from the moment the order was given till the shell was heard going over. The time taken was duly reported to Division, and woe betide any battery commander whose battery took more than thirty seconds. However, there were ways and means of circumventing even the wiliest of brass-hats. A good liaison officer would find out the time and place where the infantry proposed having the day's test. The officer would then warn the telephonists and the battery. A spare signaller would watch for the approach of the infantry officer, the battery would be told to " hold on," another signaller standing at the exit of the battery telephone dug-out, and a gunner with his hand on the firing lever of the particular gun laid on the trench the infantry had selected for the test. And thus the round was on its way almost before the infantry officer could turn round to listen for it. And then we would all go to sleep again, or resume our game of bridge or crown and anchor, happy and thankful at having cheated Olympus once more. A certain battalion, with whom we were always the very best of friends (it need not be further specified than that they were in the 55th Infantry Brigade), wishing to do us a good turn, as they thought, reported once that we had taken only five seconds to do the test. It was unfortunate that in this particular case the time of flight of the shell from the gun to where it passed over our front line was $7\frac{1}{2}$ seconds, so they had been too kind! It became the joke of the Division for a time, and General Metcalfe used to twit us on the remarkable performance of one of our guns! If these tests did not speed up possible infantry calls for fire in the way the brass-hats intended, it certainly made battery commanders more adept in the art of " wangling." When all one's plans broke down, and there was a regrettable and reprehensible delay in getting the round off, it was always possible to state in the report, which was sure to be called for, that the round had been a miss-fire or a premature!

CHAPTER IV.

The following are extracts from some of the weekly reports that were sent in during the next six months :—

5.12.15.—Twenty-three rounds of "A" (shrapnel) fired this week. An electric night aiming-point light has been made by the fitter for use in case of night firing.

12.12.15.—2nd Cheshire Brigade R.F.A. (T.F.) sent four officers and twelve telephonists and six sergeants to be attached to A/84 for instruction on their arrival in France.

19.12.15.—The A.D.V.S. has reported very favourably on the condition of the battery's horses.

26.12.15.—An unusually large party, 120, of Germans was observed at Marlboro' Wood. (Note.—These were spotted by Bdr. Steptoe.)

2.1.16.—The battery canteen (at the wagon line) is in full working order, and much patronised.

9.1.16.—D/168 brigade R.F.A. attached for instruction, occupying our alternative position.

17.1.16.—Fired on a party of seventeen enemy near Bunny Wood, causing several casualties. (Note.—These also were observed by Bdr. Steptoe.)

23.1.16.—Germans exploded three mines near Tambour du Clos (near Fricourt). No damage done.

31.1.16.—Gas alarm. Faint smell of gas (?) in the air.

6 & 7.2.16.—Relieved in action by " T " Battery R.H.A. Marched back to Buire. Gun drill and signalling classes started.

20.2.16.—A.D.V.S. reported that the condition of the battery's horses was very good, and that they were the best in the brigade. (Note.—This sort of entry is continually occurring.)

3.3.16.—Marched to Daours and in " rest."

15.3.16.—Lieut. Gibbon broke his collar bone playing rugger. To hospital and England.

20 & 21.3.16.—Marched to Suzanne (sur Somme), and took over position in Murray Wood from A/149 Brigade R.F.A.; Major Nunn, O.C.

27.4.16.—2nd Lieut. W. G. Allen posted to 18th Divisional trench mortar battery.

28.4.16.—2nd Lieut. F. P. Schofield posted to A/84.

5 & 6.5.16.—Relieved by A/149 Brigade, and marched to wagon line at Bray sur Somme.

7.5.16.—At 2.30 a.m. started march to Argoeuves (near Amiens), 27 miles.

C

4.6.16.—Brigade sports at Argoeuves. A/84 won
all the important prizes, including
battery turnout, driving competition,
officers' open jumping, N.C.O.'s jumping, driver's led horse jumping, and
tug-of-war.

11.6.16.—Marched to Corbie and bivouacked.

12.6.16.—Marched to Bois de Tailles and
bivouacked.

16.6.16.—Went into action in Billon Wood, near
Carnoy, and prepared position for the
great offensive of 1st July, 1916.
(There is a note in the record here
which runs, " The advantage of
keeping all the horses in good condition
has been borne out lately as the teams
have had to do thirty miles a day for
many days, and over heavy going, to
bring up the large quantities of
ammunition." The work they had to
do, however, for the 1st July, 1916,
was nothing to what they were called
upon to do, *and did*, later on.)

24.6.16.—The first casualty due to enemy action.
Sergt. J. Fleming, M.M., was hit in
the arm by a splinter from a shell
near the battery. (Note.—Sergt.
Fleming was a splendid No. 1, and
made his sub-section the best in the
battery. He was respected and loved
by all his N.C.O.'s and men, whom he

> looked after as a father. He was a
> first-class horsemaster. We after-
> wards met him in 1917 in Flanders as a
> B.S.M.)

. . . . .

2nd Lieut. J. E. A. Platts joined the battery on
18th June, 1916, to replace Lieut. E. N. Dexter, who
went home sick. We were all very sorry to lose Mr.
Dexter, as he was one of the originals of 17th
October, 1914, and, besides being a keen soldier,
he was a jolly good fellow in every way. He was
an excellent horseman, and the condition of the
horses of his section (left, and afterwards centre section) testified to his ability as a horsemaster. It was
most difficult to replace him, and it is no mere compliment, but simply the bare truth, when it is said
that Lieut. Platts ably filled the vacancy till he was
wounded whilst acting as F.O.O. on Vimy Ridge on
9th April, 1917.

CHAPTER V.

THE battery had an ideal position in Billon Wood, one mile south of Carnoy. There was timber in plenty for the construction of gun-pits and dug-outs, whilst the shelter of the trees rendered detection from aircraft impossible.

We were allotted six days previous to the attack for wire cutting at 800 rounds a day. This was an unheard of rate of expenditure up to that time, and everyone enjoyed the fun, except the enemy (we hope), and our drivers, who had very little rest, having long distances to go to the A.R.P. General (now Lord) Rawlinson, the Fourth Army Commander, visited the battery position on 27th June, 1916. and praised very highly the work that had been put into it.

The O.P. was tunnelled off a communication trench running along the S. side of the Albert-Peronne road, overlooking Carnoy Valley. A high-power telescope had been lent to the battery by the National Service League, which rendered very easy accurate observation as to the damage we did to the German wire entanglements.

Great secrecy had, of course, been observed as to the actual date and hour of the attack. At last, however, the day arrived. The morning of the 1st July, 1916, was misty, and at the O.P. on the Peronne Road, from which we overlooked the Carnoy Valley, with Montauban on the right, and

Mametz on the left, it was feared the observers there would not see the actual attack. However, a few minutes before 7.30 a.m., zero time, the mist thinned, and those who were lucky enough to be on duty at the O.P. were able to see the 7th Queen's, whom we were covering, and the 8th East Surreys on their right, forming up in front of their trenches. The battery were very delighted to be supporting the 7th Queen's, for ever since the early days of combined training in England we had looked upon this battalion as our own particular infantry. The best of good feeling had always existed between the personnel of the two units, especially the two officers' messes.

The long line of men formed up in front of our front line was a wonderful sight, and only eclipsed as one saw them go across No Man's Land. The 8th East Surreys led off with a football, which incident is now famous history.

Lieut. R. Darley acted as our F.O.O. on this occasion, and performed very useful and meritorious work. Finding the Queen's were held up at a trench called Montauban Alley, for want of bombs, he made his way back to the Battalion H.Q., reported the matter, and led back a party with bombs. The attack was then successfully pushed forward to its allotted objective. Bombardier T. McMillan and Trumpeter A. P. Olney performed excellent work in keeping up communication with the F.O.O., the O.P., and the battery.

It was on the Divisional front, and on the edge of the " lane " allotted to A/84 that a German machine gunner was found chained to his M.G. in his concrete covered emplacement—to prevent him running away. However, this fellow was a stout and brave soldier, for he would not surrender, and had to be shot, having caused considerable casualties to our infantry long after the attack had passed beyond him.

The German counter barrage was very weak and thin, and came down on and behind our front line before zero hour. After half-an-hour it stopped, except for a few H.V. shells.

It should here be recorded that this was the first occasion on which the " creeping barrage " was employed by the British artillery. It was the outcome of trench warfare in excelsis, and was made possible by the large increase in the number of guns the New Armies provided, together with an enormously augmented supply of shells. Like other successful innovations, the creeping barrage was used in and out of season, on every possible and needless occasion. It became the sine quâ non of every platoon raid, and was frequently the only artillery expression the infantry, from the divisional major-general down to the battalion orderly room clerk, seemed to know; and certainly all they understood as to the rôle of the guns.

Things went very well on the XIII. Corps' front, both the 18th Division and the 31st Division on our right securing all their objectives from Montauban to Mametz. On the left, however, Mametz Wood held up the advance and delayed matters. Further on to the left, rumour had it one division (one of the thirties) was so full of rum that it could not go over the top ! This holding up destroyed all hope of a great break through, and the retreat of the enemy to the Rhine.

The battery remained at Billon Wood, and was still able to fire at long range. However, on 8th July we advanced to a position in the old German front line, called Breslau Point, in Carnoy Valley.

From here we supported attacks on our left to capture Mametz Wood. We were fortunate in escaping many casualties here, although we were worried at times with attentions of an 8in. howitzer.

On July 14th, the ground in front of the two villages of Bazentin Le Grand and Le Petit was taken, and later in the day the battery commanders rode forward with Lieut.-Col. Blois to select positions in Caterpillar Valley. It was on the way back from this reconnaissance that Col. Blois was mortally wounded, on the Montauban Road, by a shell exploding underneath his horse. He died the same evening in hospital at Daours. Sergt. Alford's tribute, " He was a gentleman," truly described him —he was a gentleman in every sense of the term. Possibly some may have felt that the Colonel was not at all times the most lovable of men, yet he was without question a splendid soldier, absolutely fair, and unusually just, and he always " backed up " his battery commanders. Colonel Blois's going was a great loss, and was deeply felt by everyone. After the lapse of a few days he was succeeded by Lieut.-Col. H. Cornes, D.S.O.

The spirit of the offensive and of open warfare had been so stimulated in the battery that this new position in Caterpillar Valley was occupied by a field movement. We advanced at the trot along the bottom of the valley in battery column, and when opposite the position the orders, " Sections right wheel," " Gallop," were given. Though the latter order was hardly allowed by strict adherence to F.A.T., it reflected the spirit of the way in which the battery had been trained.

It was here that the battery received its first real smell of poison gas, necessitating the use of gas masks.

On 15th July, 1916, the two Bazentins were taken, in the attack on which we fired our first shots from our new position. No previous registration had been carried out, for fear of giving this advanced position away. On this day also started the numerous and unsuccessful attacks on Delville Wood. On one day alone, 18th July, the battery fired the creeping barrage through the Wood six times, but, notwithstanding these many attacks, the enemy remained in possession.

The bringing up of ammunition was most unpleasant and unhealthy work, as Caterpillar Valley was full of batteries. The enemy, knowing this, fairly plastered the valley with shells of every calibre.

However, on 23rd July, 1916, we were withdrawn and, marvellous to relate, we cleared the position of its 1,700 rounds, and got the guns away without a casualty. The wagon line had been brought up to the old battery position at Billon Wood, where we picked it up, and marched to the Bois de Tailles. Next day we started on our journey North. Partly by train and partly by road, via Aubigny, Liercourt (the scene of a *very* convivial evening by a combined officers' mess), and Pont Remy, we reached the Armentieres front. Here we took over a wonderful position at L'Armée, two miles from Armentieres. Our guns, in good pits, with excellent platforms, were in the garden of a house in which, and in neighbouring ones, we lived in comfort. For three weeks we were in clover. Not much firing or other work to do, and plenty of time to visit Armentieres, which was then very little knocked about and full of everything desirable.

In this position we fired, from one gun, twenty-two properly layed and observed rounds in one minute, in a brigade competition. " B " sub-section created this record. It was in this position also that we "scrounged" our first "battery trap." The saddler made up some suitable harness, and it was used by the officers, B.S.M., and one or two other privileged persons, to drive to near-by centres of attraction. On marches this trap was very useful to carry extra kit—somehow or other the B.S.M. looked upon it as *his* kit carrier!

The wagon line was also in a delightful place, near Erquinghem. The only thing that worried the officer-in-charge and the B.S.M. was the annoying habit of the brass hats and the medical fraternity in coming round and looking for flies! Woe betide any wagon line that hadn't a fly proof meat safe, and sanitary accommodation of the approved fly proof construction! Still, an evening at the " pictures," or elsewhere, in Armentières, made up for even these trials.

After three glorious weeks here we marched back to the Somme.

On 1st September, 1916, the battery went into an unprepared position near Ovillers La Boiselle with the wagon line on the Brickfields at Albert. From here we took part in the capture of the famous Wunderwurk near Thiepval.

On 23rd September, 1916, the battery moved over to a position below Contalmaison, and supported the Canadians. This was the first time we had been with the Canadians, and both on this occasion and when we were afterwards attached to them we were much impressed with their capacity for "getting things done," not only from a fighting point of view, but also from an administrative, together with an absence of red tape and pettifogging staff regulations.

From this position we assisted in the capture of Courcelette, on 15th September, 1916, when tanks were used for the first time. We then advanced to S.W. of Pozieres. From here, on 2nd October, 1916, we went over to Blighty Wood, or to give it the official name, Authuille Wood, east of Albert. Here a very snug position was built in a bank. " One of the best built and tidiest positions I have seen since the 1st July," said General Jacobs, the II. Corps commander, when visiting us. On 9th October, 1916, we fired in the barrage for the capture of Stuff Redoubt by the 55th Infantry Brigade, while on 14th October we assisted in the recapture of Schawben Redoubt. During the remainder of October, and most of November, we were continually answering S.O.S. calls in consequence of attacks by the enemy on these two famous Redoubts. Difficulties, owing to the soft and muddy nature of the front area, were now beginning to be experienced in bringing up gun ammunition. Teams had to be reinforced, and only limbers used. A suggestion to provide ammunition carriers for horses was sent in to Division from A/84 as an alternative method of bringing up ammunition; and it is curious to note that shortly afterwards ammunition carriers for horses were for the first time issued to the B.E.F. The design, though different in a few details, was practically identical with that suggested by A/84!

Ground, such as Wretched Way, Lucky Way, and Hansa Line, was taken before the 2nd December, 1916, when we came out of action.

Various congratulatory and complimentary messages were received during this strenuous and trying period from II. Corps, 18th and 39th Divisions, and the 18th and 39th Divisional Artillery commanders, expressing their appreciation of the gunners' work.

Before we marched back to " rest," however, the great re-organisation took place. As from 1st December we were turned from a four-gun battery into one of six guns. This was accomplished by the breaking up of the original C/84, and one section coming to A/84, and the other to B/84. A new C/84 joined us as the result of the breaking up of a brigade in the 11th Divisional Artillery in January, 1917. In the same way we welcomed to the brigade a six-gun 4.5in. howitzer battery from the 52nd (Lowland) Division; the old D/84 being split up between the howitzer batteries of the 82nd and 83rd Brigades of the 18th Division.

Lieut. F. J. Rice, who was second in command of the battery, now left us to become captain of C/82 Bde. R.F.A. His going was a real loss to the battery.

Captain (as he then was) Paterson joined A/84 as second in command, and Lieut. Walter Taylor came with his section from C/84. With him came also B.Q.M.S. Ridout, B.Q.M.S. A. Lewer now leaving us to join the 84th B.A.C. Sixty other ranks, two guns and limbers, four ammunition wagons complete, 35 horses and ten mules came in the section from C/84.

Only one day, 3rd December, was allowed units to shake down and O.C.'s, B.S.M.'s. and B.Q.M.S.'s to get some idea of their new responsibilities. Early on 4th December, 1916, we marched to Authieule, and on the next day to Beaumetz, and arrived at Grand Laviers, a village three miles west of Abbeville, on 6th December. Here, in more or less comfortable quarters, we prepared to spend Christmas, 1916, our second in France.

The country around was scoured for pigs, turkeys and chickens, which Venneear, Smith and Thomas

cooked in their usual admirable style for the troops.
A supply of English beer was secured, and a hearty
Christmas dinner was enjoyed by all. The sergeants'
mess had a regal feast, the only trouble being that
Sgt. Last would insist on continuing to sing, and
Sgt. Alford aided and abetted him! In the officers'
mess also there was not much evidence of bully beef
or ration limejuice. As on the Christmas Days of
1914 and 1915, everybody in the battery received a
present of a muffler, pair of gloves, pipe or cigar-
ettes—the gifts of friends of the battery at home.

Abbeville provided all sorts of amusements, whilst
a house with green shutters also provided relaxations
for the soldier wearied with five months' hard fighting on the Somme!

A rather amusing incident, if embarrassing,
occurred here. One night a Frenchman came to the
officers' mess and said the major was urgently needed
at his house. Further enquiries elicited the information that his wife was about to present him with a
baby. He had confused the English word " major "
with the French " médecin-majeur." Needless to
say, the major referred him to the brigade medical
officer. A gunner is supposed to be able to turn his
hand to anything, but it is not believed the War
Office issue a handbook on gynæcology.

But the war still continued, and we had to go
back into action. On 2nd January, 1917, we left
Grand Laviers, and marched to Beauvoir Riviére,
on the 3rd January to Mezerolles, on the 4th January
to Authieule, and arrived at our new wagon line at
Bouzincourt on the 5th January. The gun position
was in a horrible spot, an old, falling-to-pieces, and
fearfully wet and muddy position, a few hundred
yards in front of the one we had vacated before
Christmas, half-way between Blighty Wood and

Nab Junction. There was practically no cover, even
against the weather, and consequently many fellows
went down with trench fever before the position
could be improved. These unfortunate fellows included Tptr. A. P. Olney. He always tried to get
up to the gun line as a signaller, and thoroughly
enjoyed, or seemed to, a day in Stuff Redoubt, at
our O.P. there. It was not a very healthy spot, for
the enemy periodically shelled it, and the approach
to it was even more unsatisfactory. But " Tich "
Olney was one of the pluckiest and gamest young-
sters imaginable. He enlisted, direct into the battery,
in 1914, whilst only sixteen.

It was at this period that " calibration " and
" meteor telegrams " came into practical use. These
refinements, and sometimes seemingly contradictory
results of theory and practice, led to a certain amount
of confusion at first. Certain officers of the battery
will recollect how one of these "misunderstandings"
looked like having serious consequences, of the Stel-
lenbosch variety, had not the Corps G.O.C. R.A.,
Brig.-General Geddes, been a kind-hearted and
human friend of the battery.

After ten days we advanced to a much better
position, close to Nab Junction, on the left of
Mouquet Farm. We were still covering the 61st
Division in front of Grandcourt. A sharp frost
now set in, and helped the enemy considerably when
he began his great strategical retreat from the
Somme. The ground froze so hard that it even
bent the points of pickaxes when struck. Night
after night the mercury went down to 0° F. Everything froze, even the plum-and-apple jam on the
breakfast table! The wagon line was at Senlis,
and but for Capt. Paterson's untiring efforts, many
men and horses would have " gone down," first in

the mud, and afterwards in the cold. In spite of
his work in improving billets and horse standings,
many had to give up the struggle and " go sick."
Amongst these was Sgt. Last, one of the battery's
originals in 1914. The cold proved too much for
his rheumatism, and so he eventually got back to
England. He had been one of our greatest assets
in teaching riding and horsemanship, and was
always able to take the B.S.M.'s place when necessary. He was the best horseman the battery ever
had, and was genuinely respected by all ranks.

The great German retreat on the Somme started
on 6th February, 1917; on that morning our infantry
found that the enemy had vacated Grandcourt during the night. This retreat is described as one of
the enemy's most brilliant and successful operations
during the whole war. General Ludendorf certainly
thinks so (vide " Memoirs " by Gen. Ludendorf).
For the next three weeks the 18th Division was very
busy trying to hurry the Germans in going back.
During this period barrages were fired for attacks
on Grandcourt Trench, Coffee Trench, Boom
Ravine, and South Miraumont Trench.

After failing to take the left section (under Lt.
R. K. A. Kennedy, who had joined the battery on
22nd January, 1917) forward with teams, owing
to the perfectly impossible state of the ground, the
section was pushed forward to Desire Trench, on
24th February, on a light railway, which had been
laid. Lt. Kennedy made his men as comfortable as
conditions allowed, though all he had to do it with
was mud, mud, mud, and any odd material he could
collect from the old German trenches. Still, he
did it.

After Boom Ravine had been taken, a position
near the head of it was chosen for the battery. To

get the guns there, however, a long detour through Grandcourt and Miraumont had to be made. Perhaps the most brilliant tactical piece of work the battery ever did was in occupying this position. In order to reach it, the West Miraumont Road, which was in front of the position, had to be used. This road, or the remains of it, was in full view of the enemy, and was thus ordered to be used only at night. Several batteries tried to get up it, but all got stuck in the mud and shell holes. When A/84 passed up the road, we counted twelve temporarily abandoned guns belonging to other units. The night of 3/4 March, 1917, was misty, which added to the trouble. A/84, seeing the impossibility of getting up the hill in the dark, waited for dawn ; remaining outside Miraumont. At the first suspicion of dawn the ascent was begun. Nos. 1 skilfully leading and drivers superbly driving their horses, the battery literally galloped up the hill. The mist only just held till the last gun reached cover at the top. A/84 was the only battery which got all its guns up into action at the first attempt. It may have been more good luck than good judgment in relying on there being time to get the battery up the exposed hill between dawn and the rising of the mist, but it was good driving, pure and simple, that got the guns up. To help those who took part in it to recall that advance, and for others to visualise some of the difficulties, it may be mentioned that one abandoned gun of another battery had to be actually driven over by our teams ! A huge effort was asked of the battery, and they accomplished it. The battery, and the only battery, was there ready to support its infantry.

The drivers will never forget the appalling difficulties in bringing ammunition on pack animals up

Boom Ravine. Many a good "hairy" had to be
mercifully shot there, having sunk up to its neck in
the terrible mud from sheer exhaustion. It was an
awful existence for the gunners, too—mud every-
where were there was not water. And yet they kept
their guns clean and bright.

The weather improved at last, and the enemy
continued his retreat. We advanced through Irles
on 17th March, 1917, to which the enemy gave a
farewell bombardment an hour before we went
through to take up a position a mile to the south-east

At times we were out of touch with the enemy,
and information of his position was always scrappy.
One day Lt. Schofield and the O.C. were walking
forward in the area in front of Loupart Wood,
thinking the enemy had retreated that morning as
he was supposed to be doing, "according to plan."
A small party of the 7th Queen's were observed by
these two wanderers under the lee of the bank of a
sunken road coming out of Bihucourt. Thinking
they might have some later information, our two
strollers went across an open field to them, 300 yards
off. On being asked if they had any idea where
the enemy were, the patrol whispered, "There's a
Jerry M.G. 30 yards over there," pointing over the
bank. "We daren't show our heads, and we had
a sweepstake on as to the number of yards away
from here you two would be hit!" How those two
officers *crawled* away!

The wagon line was advanced to the valley south-
east of Irles, about a quarter of a mile behind the
battery. Everything was got ready for open warfare, and a long advance. But nothing eventuated.
The country, as far forward as Ervillers, was reconnoitred for possible gun positions. But on 22nd
March, 1917, we withdrew from action, and marched

back to Senlis. An interesting proof that the battery's horses were still in good condition, in spite of their very trying and strenuous existence during the last three months, was evidenced during this withdrawal. There was a very steep hill, with a sharp corner in it at Irles, and it took some units several hours to get their guns and vehicles up. But A/84's horses pulled all their wheels up without a stop or hitch ; two teams even going back to lend a hand to another battery !

CHAPTER VI.

THE Brigade's withdrawal from action on 22nd March, leaving the rest of the 18th Divisional Artillery in action, marked yet another milestone in its existence. Since the last artillery reorganisation in December, 1916, each Division had had three artillery brigades. Now, yet another reorganisation was made. In future there were to be only two brigades in a divisional artillery, the third one becoming an army brigade, available for attachment to any division, corps, or army needing reinforcement in field artillery. Being the junior brigade of the 18th Divisional Artillery since the break up of the 85th Bde. last December, it fell to the 84th to become an Army Brigade. These brigades earned weird names—" Legion of the Lost," " Travelling Circus," " Storm Troop," " Flying Column," and others not so polite. At first we were " Nobody's Children," and we were " done down " by every division and corps we were attached to, and given all the dirty jobs to do and all the rotten positions to occupy. The 51st (Highland) Division must be excepted from this charge, however. Later on it was realised that army brigades were always fighting, and deserved rather more consideration. And so the pendulum swung to the opposite side, and we became the pets of every corps we were in, and divisions took the tip and treated us as one of their own brigades.

From Senlis, on 23rd March, we marched to Rubempré, on the 24th to Gezaincourt (where Lieut.

Platts rejoined us from hospital), on the 25th to Sibiville, and arrived at Frevin Capelle on 26th March, 1917. Three other army brigades (23rd, 64th, and 315th) were also marching on the same road from the Somme.

The brigade had been brought up to help in the concentration of artillery for the attack on Vimy Ridge, and we were attached to the 51st (Highland) Division for this purpose.

The wagon line was in a farm at Frevin Capelle, and here the whole battery remained till 29th March. It was a very muddy spot, and Capt. W. Taylor (who had been promoted to be captain of the battery on Capt. Paterson leaving to take command of C/83), had a most difficult task in keeping horses and personnel as dry as possible. Picquet posts and timber were very hard to come by, and Lieut. Kennedy, who was at the wagon line with Captain Taylor, spent whole days touring the countryside with a wagon in search of material.

The gun position was 300 yards from the ruined village of Ecurie, and 900 yards from our front line. It had been very partially dug by the 64th Army Bde., merely a shallow trench and embrasures. Owing to its exposed position in this forward area little digging could be done, as otherwise the position might have been given away to enemy aerial observers. We were ordered to register, and this gave the enemy the necessary hint of a battery in action. However, poor B/84, who were 300 yards behind us, were the unfortunate people selected by the German counter-battery. The one stray whizz-bang that did land on the position very unfortunately wounded Driver C. Riach, who had been the Major's faithful servant since 14th October, 1914. He went home, only to come out again to be killed by a bomb near Vlamertinge in the autumn. He was the most faithful and loyal fellow possible— a true Scot.

The zone allotted to the battery was to the north of Roclincourt, and the O.P. was in a communication trench to the south of this village.

Until the 9th April, 1917, the battery took part, daily, in systematic bombardments of the German trench system. Four hundred rounds a day was our average consumption. Besides making good this large expenditure, a store of over 3,000 rounds had to be accumulated. The teams had to go right back to Acq, a distance of some 20 miles altogether, to collect ammunition. It usually took 10-12 hours for a team to do this. This meant the drivers had very little sleep and were hardly ever dry. They certainly had a far worse time than the gunners.

Work on improving the strength of the position being inadvisable, the gunners had plenty of time on their hands. When the " red devils " of Fokkers would allow movement, football was played just behind the position. There have not been many occasions when it has been possible to play football within three-quarters of a mile of the enemy. A large number of hares were in the vicinity, and Sergt. O'Brien endeavoured to make the officers' mess compound a felony in their accepting some of the results of his prowess with a rifle!

The attack on the 9th April, 1917, started at 5.30 a.m., and the battery continued firing till after 1 p.m., firing 35 barrages in the main attack, and answering numerous calls for assistance in repelling enemy counter-attacks.

The barrage for the great attack started to the second, all guns along the Front seeming to open fire simultaneously. It was one of the best

synchronisations we experienced, being bettered only
by the opening of the Messines barrage.

Lieut. J. E. A. Platts was our F.O.O., and was,
unfortunately, hit in the arm by a piece of a 5.9in.
soon after the start of the battle. He gallantly
stuck to his job, and would not go to the dressing
station till relieved of his duties by another officer.
We were all very sorry to lose him, especially his
section—the centre—which he had got to a high
state of efficiency. Lieut. R. K. A. Kennedy succeeded him as section commander.

The battle of Vimy Ridge was, as everyone
knows, a brilliant success the first day, but the mud
again delayed the advance of the British artillery,
and so gave the enemy the time he needed to re-
organise. We advanced on 12th April to a position
near Thèlus, and occupied it till the front line was
close to Oppy and Arleux, and Gavrelle. On 24th
April, 1917, the right and centre sections of the
battery advanced to the most ill-fated position the
battery ever occupied, called The Tunnel, behind the
railway embankment near Bailleul, near Lens. It
was named the Tunnel position as there was a narrow
tunnel, for pedestrian traffic only, under the embankment, just on the left of the position. This tunnel
was the battery's sole shell-proof cover; indeed, but
for it every human being at the guns must have
been killed.

The left section, which remained near Thèlus
for the first attack on Oppy, had to fire at a long
range. In the final barrage, at 8,800 yards, each
gun fired 100 rounds at 20 seconds to one minute
interval between rounds. The buffers were spring
buffers, fitted with auxiliary oil tanks. Fitter
Wetten hovered round each gun in turn, but his
preliminary work had been so good that they both

kept in action all through. A most creditable
performance.

The two sections at the Tunnel were not to open
fire till Oppy Wood was taken, as the position was
very exposed. However, the wood was not taken,
and though we never actually fired a round from
the position, we incurred terrible casualties.

The left section joined the remainder of the guns
on 25th April.

The enemy evidently suspected the British would
place a battery in this position, as it appeared a most
suitable place, and good positions were very scarce.
The result at any rate was that the enemy plastered
the sunken road near the embankment, in which we
had started to dig shelters. Poor Gnr. Holliday, the
officers' mess cook, was the first to be killed. The
officers will always remember the marvellous way in
which he never failed to get them something hot to
eat and drink after a march or an advance. And in
an astonishly short time after arrival too. How or
where he managed to get his firewood was often a
puzzle. Sergt. Coles and Bdr. Lay (both of " D "
sub) were killed the next day; in fact, " D " sub
had four No. 1's as casualties in as many days.
Sergt. Coles was a great favourite in the sergeants'
mess, whilst Bdr. Lay was the friend of everyone,
and always willing to help a lame dog over a stile.
No matter under what conditions, he was invariably
smartly turned out, and was frequently used as an
example to the rest of the battery. His puttees,
especially, were the envy of all, in the absolutely
perfect way he rolled them. His friend, Gnr. J. C.
Steptoe, was hit at the same time, but, fortunately,
recovered in England and rejoined the battery in
October, 1917. Bdr. McMillan stopped a piece of
shell whilst bringing in his No. 1, Sgt. J. J. Jones,

who had also been hit. " Mac," as he was universally known, seemed to make a hobby of leaving our only cover and bringing in wounded fellows. Nothing daunted him, and for his splendid self-sacrificing work he was awarded the M.M.

By some wonderful means, known only to themselves, the signallers, under Corpl. Bethell, managed to keep our wires going. It entailed constantly patrolling the lines at all hours of the day and night; and not merely at all hours, but every hour—every quarter of an hour in fact.

The only piece of good fortune we had in this position was that the ammunition always managed to come up just when there was a lull in the hail of steel; and the horses and drivers got away each time before it started again. It would have meant sheer annihilation to have fought from that position, and as our casualty returns were far too large for the Staff to visit us, permission was obtained over the telephone to move " anywhere that a position can be found " ! On 26th April, in the evening, we moved to the only vacant and possible position for a battery for miles around—near Willerval. Again the teams had luck in clearing the position quickly, and during a lull. That night, 26th-27th April, 1917, everyone—officers and men—dug like furies in an old German trench some 200 yards in rear of the guns. The guns were in a semi-covered position, from which the tops of the trees in Oppy Wood (still in enemy possession) could clearly be seen. Here, again, we were not to open fire till the attack, in which it was proposed (by the General Staff) to capture Oppy, began.

It is curious how our trench, in which we lay " doggo " all day, was given away. Some German prisoners were carrying, under escort, some bombs

and S.A.A. up to our front line. They were, of
necessity, walking over the open, as there were not
any communication trenches at present. The enemy
spotted them, and, doubtless thinking they
were British, started to shell them, chasing the
prisoners and their escort to *our* trench. The enemy
battery commander saw them go to ground, and
there was no more peace for us after that. Directly
night fell we all started to dig a narrow six feet
deep trench directly behind the guns. None of us
had ever dug so fast before—or since. It was an
example of General Maxse's " intensive digging,"
with an object. The guns and thrown-up earth were
very carefully camouflaged, and movement in daylight absolutely forbidden, and so the enemy left us
in peace. Few felt like eating very much after our
recent experiences at the Tunnel, and the absence
of cooking, within 500 yards of the battery, was
not so keenly missed as it would have been under
more normal conditions.

The battle took place on 28th April, but Oppy
was a nut the British never succeeded in cracking
till the Germans voluntarily retired in 1918. The
battle of Vimy Ridge marked the time when the
enemy began to do good counter-battery work.
He had doubtless learnt the value of it from bitter
experience on the Somme.

We were spotted, by our flashes if not by direct
observation, directly the battle started, and soon we
were made aware of it. A 5.9in. laid out most of
" A " sub, and a scratch detachment consisting of
an officer, two signallers, and an officer's servant,
had to keep the gun firing its barrage. Soon after
another 5.9in. landed almost on top of " E " sub's
gun, damaging it and most of the detachment.
After peppering the ground around the battery, the

enemy quietened down till nightfall. Then began
a most unpleasant and terrible night. A 77 mm.
German battery near Lens, and at right angles to
our line of fire, began to pump in gas shells. It
had the line of our guns to an inch, and several of
the near-side gun wheels received direct hits. Sometimes these gas shells came in at the rate of 60 a
minute. A 5.9in. howitzer battery also took part
in the entertainment. Towards midnight a 'phone
message was received that the enemy were expected
to do a big raid that night. It seemed the reverse
of a cheerful prospect to man the guns whilst this
hail was on. After it had been going on, in bursts,
long and short, for several hours, a corporal suddenly rushed up to the telephonists' trench in the
centre of the battery and said " A " sub's trench
had been blown in and the detachment buried. One
of these intense bursts of gas shell was just starting,
and it appeared to be inviting certain death to
venture out to go to their possible rescue. But that
did not deter Sgt. A. J. Porter from immediately
jumping out of the trench and running to " A "
gun. On the way he was knocked over by a gas
shell, but, uninjured, he got to the blown-in trench.
Here he was joined by Bdr. Hookway. Unable to
keep under cover, and regardless of the risks they
ran, they started to dig their unfortunate comrades
out. How furiously they dug, for, perchance, Gnrs.
Piercy and Ryan might still be alive. At last, by
their untiring efforts, Piercy and Ryan were brought
out of their living graves, very exhausted by the
explosion and weight of earth on them. Porter and
Hookway gave them artificial respiration, and they
came round not much the worse for their experience.
Had Porter waited for a minute or two longer in
the telephonists' trench, in the hope the shelling

might die down, those two lives would assuredly
have been lost. It was truly "an act of God"
that saved Porter's life in his journey to "A"
sub. Both he and Hookway were very highly
recommended for this splendid act, and in due
course of time they each received the Military Medal.

And though the gun line was having such a terrible time, the wagon line also had its share of the
unpleasant things of war.

They had moved up from Frevin Capelle to near
Madagascar Corner, between Ecurie and Anzin. It
was a long and muddy trek up to the battery with
ammunition, through Thèlus and Farbus, the road
down the Ridge to the latter place being particularly
unpleasant.

On 3rd May, 1917, our troops were attacking in
the vicinity of Gavrelle, on our right. When our
attack was launched the enemy rushed up, by train
and lorry, reinforcements. From the battery O.P.
on Vimy Ridge we were actually able to see them
detraining. Of course, every battery that saw this
spectacle immediately began to range on them. It
was some time before anything successful was done,
as each battery was mistaking another unit's rounds
for its own. However, a certain amount of damage
was done, and it made the Germans run. This
fiasco led to the gunnery brass-hats writing screeds
and screeds as to who should fire, and how, in a
similar case.

Great was our joy when the Higher Command
realised, after "Z" Battery, R.H.A., had been
wiped out near by, that to keep us where we were
was useless slaughter, and so we received orders
to come back to the top of the Ridge, close to
Thèlus, on 12th May, 1917. On 15th May the guns
were pulled out to the wagon line. Here the battery

sorted itself out, and counted up its losses during
the last month. Reinforcements were received
(including Sgt. Lynn and Sgt. Hall), together with
a batch of horses.

During the battle of Vimy Ridge we had been
attached to the 51st, 31st, 2nd, and 5th Divisions.
Nearly 20,000 rounds of ammunition were fired by
the battery in this battle and the attendant operations afterwards.

On 19th May the battery marched to Hermin,
on the 20th to Amettes, on the 21st to Haverskerque
(which village we knew again twelve months later
under rather different conditions!), on 22nd to
Morbeque, and arrived at a new wagon line at
Dranoutre on 23rd May, a total march of 60 miles.
This wagon line was a delightful spot—till a few
days before the battle of Messines started. There
was cover for all the horses, huts and beds for the
men, and even a sand bath for the horses! Unfortunately, however, there was a luxurious Divisional
Headquarters in capacious and numerous huts near
by. On the night of 27th-28th May the enemy sent
over a few 30 cm. H.V. shells, intending them for
these H.Q., and making fairly good shooting. This
went on for several nights, and as the wagon line
officers' tents were, for the time being, compara-
tively immune, we naturally had many visitors
there. On the night of 31st May, however,
one shell landed on the middle wagon in the gun
park, blowing it and three others into scrap-iron,
and setting a dump of loaded ammunition boxes
on fire. Lieut. Holt did fine work in putting this
out, at imminent risk to himself. The order was
given to file the horses out, matters being further
complicated by another shell having just previously
landed in the middle of the road outside the lines.

Both before this night and afterwards our horses,
and those of neighbouring units, were usually filed
out at night into fields near by, and the lines
evacuated, for safety.   Horses on these occasions
were continually breaking loose, and it was here
that Cpl. Southwick "found " Baby! If the wagon
line was a lively place, the gun line was in clover.
Good gun pits and dug-outs had been prepared about one and three-quarters miles south-east
of Kemmel, and a light railway to bring up
ammunition from the road at Daylight Corner,
three-quarters of a mile away.   Observation,
whither we proceeded on horseback, was provided
in good shell-proof O.P.s on Kemmel Hill.   The
only fly in the ointment was that the theoretical
gunnery experts were rather trying with regard to
the correct sorting of ammunition into their various
grades.   However, as we had to fire the stuff, and
were responsible for the results, we took their beyond
perfection advice as the practical gunner usually
does. We were attached to the 36th (Ulster) Division, in the IXth Corps, and whilst great credit must
be given to them, the arrangements, down to the
minutest detail, for the battle of 7th June were
worked out to perfection by General Plumer's 2nd
Army. It is generally admitted that General Plumer
(now F.M. Lord Plumer) was our most universally
successful general on the Western Front, and certainly Messines was the most perfectly organised
show the battery was ever in.   Everything, from
first to last, went " according to plan," as Jerry
used to say.

No shell came within a quarter of a mile of the
position, and only the faintest whiffs of gas reached
us. It was the best " battle position " the battery
ever occupied, from all points of view. The O.C.
even had an open-air bath constructed for himself!

The battery came up into action on the night of
25th-26th May, 1917, and the next day registered
on Hell Farm. The wire-cutting was carried out
by the 36th Divisional Artillery, and the rôle of
the 84th Bde. was that of bombardment of selected
targets, both by day and by night. This started
on 31st May, and went on till the morning of the
battle, on 7th June, 1917. Some 6,500 rounds were
fired in this way, and 3,600 in the battle proper.
Zero hour was at 3.10 a.m. on 7th June, and consisted of 36 barrages for the battery. All objectives
on the Wytchaete Ridge were taken by the 107th
Infantry Brigade, who thanked us for an excellent
barrage.

The battery was withdrawn on the morning of
9th June, and marched to Reninghelst. On 12th
June positions for the brigade were reconnoitred
near Zillebeke Lake. The use of the word recon-
noitre rather implies that care was taken by those
composing the reconnoitring party in their reconnaissance. In actual fact this is how it was done.
The battery commanders of two brigades, with an
extra officer and two orderlies per battery, and the
two brigade commanders with their orderlies, met
the two brigade commanders (with their orderlies)
who were to be relieved, and the whole party, num-
bering 32, solemnly proceeded to walk over the
countryside! Enemy aeroplanes carefully watched
this strange party, but did not turn their gunners

on to this battalion of artillery, but carefully noted wherever directors were set up and positions apparently decided upon. We were convinced of this not long afterwards!

The famous Shrapnel Corner and Trois Rois had to be passed to approach the position selected for A/84, near the south-west corner of Zillebeke Lake. One rather amusing incident in connection with bringing up ammunition is worth recording. Lieut. Darley was the officer in charge of an ammunition convoy to the position one night before the battery came up. He got as near the position as seemed desirable, and decided to unload the G.S. wagons, loaded with boxed ammunition, and put them under the cover of a hedge. It was pitch dark, and the driver proceeded to pass Lieut. Darley the boxes, which he tumbled into a hole in the hedge. As the hole did not seem to fill up after a dozen or more boxes (representing some 50-60 rounds) had been put into it, Darley carefully looked and discovered a deep pond on the other side of the hedge! The language he gave vent to nearly set fire to the boxes at the bottom of the pond!

The guns were brought up into action on 18th June, 1917, the enemy artillery giving us a welcome on the track from Trois Rois to the position. However, no casualties were received. The ground was very low-lying and soft, and it was impossible to dig at all deeply; but we dug down as far as water —some three to four feet—and hoped for the best. A battery a few hundred yards in front of us at Blauerpoort Farm had some concrete dugouts and gunpits, but even they were not proof against the German eight-inch armour-piercing shells, for we watched them having a most awful time the next day, fully expecting it would be our turn soon.

Stirling Castle was used as a zero line, and the guns registered on it from an O.P. near Yeomanry Post.

However, we were suddenly relieved by A/113, handing our guns over to them on the position, and taking over theirs in the wagon line. The enemy gave us a warm parting, and chased the last party to leave all the way down the track to Trois Rois.

On 22nd June, 1917, we marched to Houtkerque, near Poperinghe. Here we had a real rest, even the Staff not bothering us! The battery was under canvas, and the weather delightful. However, the authorities were only fattening us up for the next battle, so we made the most of the time. " Pop." had then not been much knocked about, and " Mrs. Cyril's " and " Skindle's," not to mention the officers' club, were frequently patronised by all the officers ; the N.C.O.'s and men finding equally-desirable places of refreshment and amusement.

Battery commanders were always being asked by their officers, " Can I go and see the D.A.D.O.S. (or I.O.M.) about something this afternoon, sir ? " B.C.'s being people of average intelligence would smile to themselves as they answered, " Yes." Then the officer would say, " As D.A.D.O.S.'s office is so close to Pop., would you mind if I didn't come back till late to-night ? "

It is suspected that the D.A.D.O.S. did not receive one-tenth of the number of visitors who had so declared their intention of calling on that stony-hearted official. It is quite possible that even battery

commanders visited Pop., after loudly declaring in
the mess and to their B.S.M. that they were going
to see Corps H.Q.! A discreet groom is worth
his weight in gold, or in five-franc notes. Many
officers, and N.C.O.'s too, can vouch for the truth
of this, after visiting Pop., Westoutre, Armentieres,
Amiens, or Caudry.

Working parties were sent up on 29th June to
prepare a position at Bluet Farm, on the road between Elverdinghe and Boesinghe. We were to
occupy this for the great Flanders attack of 31st
July, 1917, the start of the sad and terrible Paschendaele fight.

We were attached to the Guards' Division, in the
XIVth Corps. We went up into action on 14th July,
and lay next to C/74 of the Guards' Division artillery.

An interesting incident happened on 20th July.
The O.C. the battery happened to be the sole officer
on the position that morning, and was struggling
with belated " returns " in his dugout. Suddenly
an orderly runs up and says, " There's a general
coming, sir ! " The O.C. crammed on a tin hat,
grabbed up a box-respirator, and rushed out to
welcome (?) a brigadier, followed by a good-looking
young staff captain. The B.G. received a most
regimental salute from the O.C., who was informed
that " they " would like to see round the position.
Generals are usually in the habit of using, and
perhaps repeating, the pronoun " I." The young
staff captain took the keenest interest in having the
principles of the new air-recuperator gun we had

just received explained, and in all the details of a battery position. The B.G. seemed quite content to remain silent in the background.

Somehow or other, the face of this staff captain seemed familiar to the battery commander, but he was unable to definitely place him. Directly they had gone, after having had a whisky-and-soda in the mess, it flashed across the O.C. that it was the Prince of Wales who had been the interested staff captain. This surmise was subsequently confirmed. The O.C. afterwards met him near the O.P. at Cheapside. The Prince was and is a good sportsman, and refused to take advantage of his birth ; this often caused the authorities concern, as he insisted on seeing things for himself, no matter the danger. There is the story that in the first days of the war he was worrying Lord Kitchener to let him go out to the front, but Lord K. said "No." The Prince persisted, and said, "What does it matter if I am killed? I've got brothers." The field marshal replied, "It wouldn't matter in the least if you were killed, but it would be very awkward if you were captured!"

The enemy left us alone in our position, though he periodically "hated" Bluet Farm.

The battery had a large amount of night firing to do, on roads and communication trenches, but we always contrived to fire only when another battery in the vicinity was also firing. We hoped thus to deceive the enemy flash-spotters and sound-rangers. This system would not have deceived the British detectors, but it is a fact that whenever we were in a position from which we could carry out this principle, the enemy never strafed us.

E

The great 31st July, 1917 came, and the Guards
Division did splendidly. But as this is not a history of the war, but only that of A/84, the narra-
tive will be confined to the doings of the battery.
After firing 28 lifts in the attack, the battery advanced at 8.30 a.m. to a position close to the Yser
Canal, west of Boesinghe. We had orders to advance to the canal first, and perhaps later in the
day to cross it and take up the advance. But the
Fates willed otherwise, and we remained in the canal
position for a week. The great break through had
not taken place, but the Higher Command hoped
it might yet, if the attack was pressed. And so, on
7th August, 1917, we advanced to a position on the
north-east edge of Artillery Wood, by the ruined
village of Pilchem. The guns were got along the
badly smashed-up roads by our splendid " hairies,"
the help of drag-ropes, and much hectic language !

Ammunition was brought up by pack animal, and
it was an unhealthy job coming up the road past
Steam Mill. The wagon line moved up to Elverdinghe, and suffered casualties from H.V. guns ;
whilst the B.A.C., behind our lines, were worried
even more. The gun line began to suffer severe
casualties. Corporal A. F. Bethell, M.M., and
Fitter Wetten were killed, and many went down
with wounds. Poor Bethell had his thigh fractured
by a splinter, and died at the C.C.S. at Canada
Farm, behind Elverdinghe, being buried at the
cemetery there. Though he must have been in
frightful pain, he smiled as he was being carried
away to the dressing station on a stretcher, and
told us " not to worry about him." The very effi-

cient and reliable signalling staff the battery had
always possessed was chiefly due to his untiring
hard work, and his death was a sore blow to his
fellow-signallers and many friends.

On account of the exceedingly trying time we
had been experiencing, we were relieved on 12th
August, 1917, by the 84th Battery R.F.A., and
went back for ten days' "rest" to St. Momelin,
near St. Omer ; exchanging guns till we returned.
Visits to St. Omer, and the absence of "crumps"
soon made us cheerful, though the enemy made a
big air raid one night on St. Omer. St. Momelin
was at a safe distance from the city, but it was
dreadful to even war-tried soldiers like the battery
to see the panic of the poor peasants.

Returning on 22nd August, we took over our
old position on the Pilkhem Ridge from the 84th
Battery, who had worked hard on it, and had put in
some dugouts. The enemy left us more alone now,
and transferred their attentions to D/84, who were
fifty yards behind us. Even this had its unplea-
santnesses for us, though, for "D" had a lot of
gas shells dumped between them and us ; and if the
wind was from them when the enemy was shelling
them, we quite expected to be gassed with our own
poison should the dump be hit. Both "B" and
"C" batteries on our left had a very thin time, and
suffered many casualties.

One of the battery's unpleasant duties here was
to prepare a position right forward, in view of an
expected advance. This new position was situated
on the Steenbeek, near Langemarck. Work could
only be done in the very early morning, owing to

the hostile aeroplanes, whilst the footbridges across the Steenbeek were favourite targets for the enemy's night-firing batteries. Fortunately we did not have to occupy this position. During this period the battery was firing at the rate of 300 rounds per twenty-four hours.

On 27th September, 1917, the battery moved to a position at Admiral's Cross Roads, north of Wieltje, relieving A/155. We were now under the XVIIIth Corps, and 48th Division.

Here we had to prepare a forward position, also, curiously enough, on the Steenbeek, but just on the outskirts of the north end of St. Julien. All that remained of what must once have been a pretty little village, was a few half and several completely wrecked concrete pillboxes.

It was on 29th September that Lt. G. W. Clutter-buck, who was attached to the battery, was gassed at the O.P. 700 yards in front of Admiral's Cross Roads.

On 3rd October, 1917, the guns were taken forward to the St. Julien position. It was quite impossible to dig more than six inches deep without coming to water, and the dug-outs (in name only) consisted of shelters erected against the sides of a small ex-enemy pillbox (which had its one entrance facing the enemy, of course), into which the whole gun-line personnel used to crowd, and passing strangers as well, when some enemy battery commander decided on a strafe.

The 18th Divisional Artillery came and took up positions around St. Julien until they moved up to Poelcapelle. This was the first time we had seen

our " relations " since we had become an army
brigade.   The country, from the O.P.'s Victoria
and Genoa (two ex-German pillboxes, the latter,
by the way, being situated where the British front
line in 1914 was), was extraordinarily difficult to
pick up and register the guns on, as it was all turned
into brown mud and water by the millions of shells,
British and German, which had been fired. Trenches
were quite impossible to pick out, not that there
were many, consolidated shell-holes being the infantry's home chiefly.   Consequently, a large amount
of the shooting done was " by map," and the captured German returns of casualties and their des-
criptions of the havoc our artillery fire caused are
ample testimonies to the accuracy of our guns and
ammunition, to say nothing of the exactness of the
corrections and calculations for atmospheric changes
worked out at the battery.   The eternal receivings
of the apparently meaningless masses of figures
composing the meteor messages must have been one
of the bugbears of a telephonist's life :—6067, 75269,
etc., etc.

From St. Julien the battery was pushed forward
—the first, as usual—to Spot Farm, in front of St.
Julien. How the guns were ever dragged, not over
roads, but over mere morasses, was a marvel. A section was taken up on 24th October to render close
support for the attack on Wallemolen, and the credit
for getting these guns up must be given to the marvellous energy and dogged perseverance of Lt.
Darley.   The journey of the detachments (only a
guard was at present with this section, no accommodation having yet been built) from the main posi-

tion at St. Julien to Spot Farm on the early morning of 26th October, prior to the attack starting,
was through a regular inferno.   Gas shells were
dropping all along the duckboards, and only the
heavy rain drowned the gas-laden atmosphere.
Eventually the whole six guns were got up.   Shelters were built around the few concrete boulders, the
remains of the enemy pillbox named Spot Farm.
The battery had ranged on this very place when in
action at Admiral's Cross Roads !   It is quite impossible for words to describe how anyone lived
here, or remained alive ; actual experience is necessary to appreciate it.   An army composed of men
who could stand, withstand, and still stand, such
awful conditions, in the spirit in which the N.C.O.'s
and gunners of A/84 did, was bound to win this,
or any war.   Casualties were very heavy, including
2nd Lt. F. W. Horn (wounded thigh), who had
only just joined us ; and one of the saddest and at
the same time most gallant incidents in the battery's
history occurred here.   The road from St. Julien
to the gun position was via a corner called Winni-
peg, some 500 yards off.   This was the only way up
for pack-animals ; and we at the battery were, on
24th November, watching a party of ten to fifteen
pack animals being led up with ammunition.   When
about 800 yards away from the position, the enemy
began to " hate " the road with 5.9in. shells with
instantaneous fuses.

We were unable to recognise to which battery, and
there were several near, the convoy belonged, but
we could see the awful time they were having.   One
of the men seemed to be directing their movements,
reversing their direction, and sending them back

towards St. Julien. We watched him helping
various drivers and frightened horses, catching
terrified horses that had broken loose, and giving
them back to their drivers. All this time the shelling
was going on, and several of the horses were hit
and killed. Eventually he had turned all his
charges, and directed them to safety, and then he,
alone, was struck down in the mud by a shell. We
who watched it could not but admire this unknown
hero who risked his life, and gave it, through stay-
ing behind to see his men away from danger. On
going over to the spot it was found that the hero
was not unknown, but was indeed our Bdr. A. J.
Pickwick. It was our own drivers and animals,
bringing up ammunition for us, that we had been
watching.

A large number of only partially successful
attacks were now taking place. Such places as Adler
Farm and Varlet Farm were taken by the 18th Division on 9th October, and the ground north-west of
Páschendaele 26th October.

During this period we were successively attached
to the 63rd (Naval) Division, 1st Canadian Division, and the 1st (Imperial) Division.

Whilst in action at Spot Farm, over 12,000 rounds
of ammunition were fired, of which more than half
was expended in night firing on communications,
etc.

The not unwelcome news that Christmas was to
be spent in " rest " was received, and we were
relieved by A/186 on 14th December, 1917. Guns
were handed over *in situ*. On 22nd December the

brigade marched to Houtkerque, and the next day
to Rubrouck, where a very merry Christmas was
spent. This was our third Christmas Day in
France, and once again we had to thank many kind
friends at home for some very thoughtful parcels
which greatly added to our enjoyment. Heavy
frost was experienced, and the slippery state of the
ground may account for the difficulty some (not
only officers) had in getting back to their billets at
night !

CHAPTER VII.

On 6th January, 1918, the battery marched back
to Mont Bernechon, and on 15th January to a very
good wagon line in the Rue de Lille, Bethune.
Most of the horses and billets were in a disused
sugar factory, the remainder being in an adjoining
horse dealer's yard. There was excellent cover here
for all horses and most of the vehicles, and separate
accommodation for the farrier, saddlers, fitters,
stores, etc. A working party, under Lieut. Kennedy,
went up on 10th January and prepared a position
near Le Touret, a mile in the rear of Festubert,
which was occupied on 23rd January, 1918. We
were first attached to the 46th Division, and afterwards to the 55th (East Lancs.) Division. The
girls' school at Festubert was the O.P. at first;
later on we shared Gun House with B/84. Several
raids took place during January and February, in
order to keep the infantry's offensive spirit up. One
very elaborately planned raid resulted in the capture,
the sole result, of a trench gas alarm bell, after an
expenditure of over 2,000 18-pounder rounds !

On 21st March, 1918, the great German offensive
started on the Cambrai front. The entire British
front was bombarded, and our sector was raided
in addition. The battery was very heavily shelled
during the whole night of 21st-22nd March with

" mustard gas " and 5.9in. H.E. On the 21st and
22nd March 40 members of the gun line were
evacuated wounded and gassed. These included
four officers, viz., Major Grant, Lieut. Holt, and
2nd Lieuts. R. Ward and Bradley. Gnr. W. Nutter
was mortally wounded by a gas shell penetrating
his dug-out and bursting inside. He was Major
Grant's servant, and never was there one who was
more loyal to his officer. The following is an
instance of his self-denying devotion. The weather
was extremely cold, and firing was very scarce
indeed. Nutter spent some hours on the 21st trying
to find wood for the brazier in the O.C.'s dug-out,
but could find none. As there was some writing
to be done and it was bitterly cold, the O.C. asked
Nutter to have yet another look round for some
firing. Five minutes later Nutter came back with
a supply, and a cheery fire was the result. It was
not till after he had been mortally hit and taken
away that his master himself discovered that this
unselfish fellow had broken up his own bed in order
to provide wood for the fire. Could one expect so
much ?

The position was strongly defended with wire
entanglements all round, Lewis gun pits, rifle em-
paulments, and platforms on which to run the guns
out for close shooting. The position was to be held to
the last in case of an attack, and the enemy would
indeed have suffered many casualties in advancing
the last 500 yards across an open field all round the
battery had he attacked and broken through. Capt.
A. M. Duff, who had joined the battery as captain
in February, commanded the guns in the absence,
in hospital, of Major Grant.

On the 28th March, however, the battery was moved over the Canal de la Bassée, and attached again to the 46th Division. This move was a fortunate one, as on the 9th April, when the Lys offensive began, the Portuguese on our immediate left gave way, and our Le Touret position became the front line. But it was not by any means all beer and skittles where the battery now was. The position was in a low-lying wood, and on the 9th April the enemy drenched the locality with mustard and phosgene gas.

Major Grant rejoined the battery from No. 14 General Hospital, Boulogne, on 7th April, 1918.

All communication broke down to the front and rear. Lieut. R. Darley and Cpl. H. Allum went out and repaired the O.P. line at great danger and risk —Signaller Kirkup was killed whilst walking along a trench with them, and died in Lieut. Darley's arms. On their return to the battery they went out again and repaired the wire to Brigade H.Q. (although it was strictly brigade's duty to keep this line in repair), thus enabling valuable information to be passed back from the O.P. For this gallant act Lieut. Darley was awarded the M.C., and Cpl. Allum the M.M.

The staunch defence by the 55th Division on our left at Festubert, and the 11th Division to whom we were now attached, prevented the enemy breaking through, but the Portuguese on the left of the 55th Division gave way and ran like hares, and the Lys Retreat commenced. A story is told that on the next day the Portuguese had a roll-call at

Boulogne of their entire army, and *all* were present
except one, and he was discovered at Le Havre!

Bethune was not now a pleasant place to be in,
with 8in. and 12in. shells dropping in and around
the wagon line. On the morning of 10th April a
12in. shell landed on the middle of "E" sub-
section's stable and made a crater 12-15 feet in
diameter, blowing the whole roof off. The horses
got loose, and when re-caught were all present except
one. They had, miraculously, hardly been touched.
The missing one could not be found, nor pieces even
seen. Then someone looked inside a knacker's cart
standing 15 yards away (this stable was in a
knacker's and sausage maker's yard), and there
was the poor animal, or what remained of it.
He had been blown clean into the cart, dead, of
course.

The German Great General Staff had calculated
to take Bethune on the morning of the 10th April,
1918, but the gallant 55th Division foiled him by
standing fast.

The wagon line moved out on the evening of
10th April, to Annezin, and bivouacked. The guns
were withdrawn on 11th April, and we marched
to Barlin, whither the wagon line moved the same
day. On 12th April we were attached to the 2nd
Canadian Division, and reconnoitred for a battery
position near Lens. In the afternoon, however,
countermanding orders were received, and we were
ordered to join the XIth Corps, north of Bethune.
So we marched back and spent the night at Auchel.
On 13th April we were attached to the 5th Division,
and a position was selected on the Aire Canal bank,

close to Ainchain Farm, and between St. Venant
and Haverskerque. The battery marched from
Auchel on the 14th April and came into action in
this position, the wagon line being at Houleron,
four miles east of Aire. There was a forward
echelon of six teams and limbers in a farm one
mile behind the guns.

Fitter Fieldhouse was killed on 16th April by one
of the very few shells which came on to this position,
and was buried at Tannay.

For a month both gun and wagon lines were in
clover. The retreat was stopped, and all (men and
horses) lived on the fat of the land. The area was
very hurriedly evacuated by the civilians, in view
of the expected German advance, leaving behind
food, wine, animals, and various useful chattels,
to say nothing of abandoned army dumps of forage
and C.C.S.'s All the officers and N.C.O.'s—and
particularly the O.C.—-looked with a blind eye when
they saw such things as a dead pig (from a Service
revolver bullet) on a stretcher being brought in to
the battery by some signallers from the O.P. Gnr.
Redfern was chief cook at the battery, and he
excelled himself in the delicacies he produced for
the troops, from ingredients supplied to him, whilst
Gnr. Hinchcliffe produced Ritz and Carlton dishes
for the officers' mess. It is believed that many of
the necessary component articles for these delicacies
came from evacuated chateaux and houses, the con-
sumers doubtless salving their consciences—but has
a soldier such an impediment ?—by thinking that if
they did not have them, who knew but that the
enemy might not be eating them on the morrow !

Wine, and good wine, there was in plenty, too; drunk out of old cut-glass wineglasses. A certain gunner brought a bottle, three-quarters full, labelled " cherry brandy," to the officers' mess, saying he had " found " it, and having drunk some he felt quite " tight." The bottle was produced after dinner that night, and all the officers declared it was the funniest cherry brandy they had ever tasted— in fact they came to the conclusion, afterwards confirmed, that it was cochineal in a cherry brandy bottle !

Very little firing was done, and with not too much to occupy anyone's time, it is feared all ranks would soon get stale, living as we were. And so the times of fresh eggs and milk for breakfast came to an end, and on 15th May we handed over this delightful position to the 112th Battery, and came out of action to the wagon line that night. At 9 a.m. on 16th May we marched to Wittes, where the cow, affectionately named " Lucille," of which the battery had become possessed through the salvaging propensities of Lieut. R. D. Taylor, was disposed of. We were indeed sorry to have fresh milk no longer, but the distance we expected to trek made the parting necessary. Let it be recorded here that the French Croix Rouge Fund benefited from the proceeds of the sale.

After spending the night at Wittes, the battery marched the next day—17th May—to Le Vielfort, near Bruay. This was a long march of 20 miles, but the horses stood it perfectly. We were bivouacked in the grounds of Le Vielfort Chateau, and after cleaning up, mounted drills took place

most days on the open ground near Bruay. The
G.O.C. 1st Corps, Sir T. Holland (nicknamed
" Butcher " Holland), inspected the brigade, and
specially picked out A/84 and complimented us
on the smart way we trotted into action, and on the
good fire control when in action.

We were also preparing for the brigade sports
which had been arranged for 9th and 10th June,
1918. B.Q.M.S. Ridout worked very hard with his
staff at getting a gun and limber and wagon and
limber into perfect condition for the " turn-out "
competition, and he was rewarded by the battery
winning first prize. B.S.M. Turner also worked
hard at training teams for the " alarm stakes " and
tug-of-war, both of which were also won. After
the sports were over and the prize-winners known,
so great was the jubilation of the battery at having
won the chief events that the prize teams, with their
guns and wagons, galloped round the arena, much
to the mortification of other competitors and the
unbounded joy of A/84-ites.

On 11th June we moved to a wagon line in
Coupigny Wood, the guns going on up into action
that night. The position was near Fosse 7, close
to the Lens-Bethune road and one mile west of Loos.
We were now attached to the 11th Division, 1st
Corps, and covered the St. Elie and Hulloch sectors.
On 22nd June the wagon line moved up to that
formerly occupied by A/59 Brigade, R.F.A., near
Hersin.

We were detailed by the G.O.C. R.A. 1st Corps
to send a section complete to the 1st Corps'
School of Instruction. This was a great compliment

to the battery's smartness and efficiency, as the
section was used at the school for instruction and
demonstration purposes for the officers and N.C.O.'s
from other units attending the school. Lieut.
S. W. W. Bell was in charge of the section at the
beginning, and later Lieut. R. K. A. Kennedy took
it over. When it had settled down it did one's
heart and eyes good to pay it a visit. Everything
was brought to the highest state of efficiency. The
harness and guns gleamed with polish and burnish,
while the horses never appeared fitter. The
personnel looked like a pre-war battery at its best,
and won much outside praise for individual keenness. Whilst too much commendation cannot be
given to the officers in charge, the hard work put in
by the N.C.O.'s and men themselves must not be
forgotten when contemplating the result.

The whole of July and the first three weeks of
August the battery remained in position near Fosse
7. Nothing much, from a fighting point of view,
took place. Trench warfare in excelsis was starting
to vegetate. " Returns " began to double and treble
in numbers. For example, a return had to be sent
in each week—and woe betide any unit that forgot
it or was an hour late in rendering it—showing (a)
the number of nails the men of the battery picked
up on the roads; (b) the number of the organised
searches made for these same nails and of how long
duration. A bright O.C. put in one of his returns :
(a) One; (b) seven searches of 24 hours' duration
each. It is not recorded whether he was court-
martialled or was awarded the O.B.E.

As the enemy was quiet, visits of inspection from senior officers and the Staff increased till all ranks hardly dared to sit down and rest for a moment.

Fresh orders arrived weekly, from our hard-worked Staff as to the equipment (down to the number of drawing pins and pencils) to be kept at all O.P.'s; and, generally, the war, as far as this front was concerned, began to get in to all manner of undesirable peace-time grooves.

On 28th July a detachment was sent by the battery to represent it in the 1st Corps' contingent that was training for the ceremonial parade held by the First Army on 4th August, 1918, at Houdain, to celebrate the fourth anniversary of the declaration of war by Great Britain on Germany. Major Grant was detailed by 1st Corps to train the whole Corps' R.A. contingent at Ruitz.

On 25th August, 1918, we pulled out and handed over the position to A/59 Bde. R.F.A. We marched the same night to a position near Annequin, which we had previously prepared. The way there took us through Vermelles, which the enemy began to shell rather heavily as we passed through its ruined streets. It says much for the steadiness of all ranks that perfect order and coolness were maintained, and the pace, a walk, was not, even unconsciously, increased. Fortunately, no casualties occurred. We were now covering the 16th (Irish) Division, though still in the 1st Corps. Rumours arrived daily, both in the form of " secret and urgent " orders and from the cookhouse, that the enemy was about to retire on this front, and various preparations were

F

made in case he did. As a matter of fact this retirement did not take place till October, after the battery had left this area.

On 8th September we were relieved by a battery of the 180th Brigade, and marched back to Le Vielfort, of pleasant memory, moving on the 10th to Le Comte. Here we were warned that we were at last going to take part in moving warfare, and so we started to shed much of our extra kit and luxuries. Drastic orders were issued that officers must not have more than the 100lb. of kit allowed them by G.R.O.; and the orders were probably carried out by no one package exceeding the stipulated amount! Great discussions and verbal fights took place between the " Q " side of the battery, who were responsible for the transport, and the " G " side, who wanted to carry our usual quantity of troughs, tarpaulins, chaff-cutters, extra blankets, battery office equipment, and the hundred and one extras and conveniences that a battery accumulates during three or four years of active service.

The battery left Le Comte on the evening of 20th September, 1918, and marched during the night to the barracks at Arras. During the march orders were received for Major D. F. Grant to proceed at once to join H.Q. R.A., 15th Division, who were now covering the front we had just left. The battery was run in his absence by Capt. E. B. Brasier-Creagh, till Major Grant rejoined on 4th December, 1918.

On 21st September the battery marched to Bapaume, on the 23rd to Halle, on the outskirts of Peronne, and on the 24th to Herville, where a wagon line was formed. The battery came into action near Brolcourt, for the assault on the Hindenburg Line, and was covering the 30th American Division, and afterwards the 25th American Division.

On 3rd October the battery supported an attack on the Beaurevoir line, which was successful. After passing through Gouy on 8th October, Serain and Elincourt on the 9th October, the battery came into action south of Maretz. Here Dvr. Gage won the M.M. by his courage in driving his wagon team under fire, and in full view of the enemy.

On 12th October the battery took part in a small operation of the 66th Division, near Le Cateau. Here operations came to a short standstill, whilst both sides recovered their breath after the unaccustomed rapid advancing and retiring.

This is a suitable point to place on record the smooth way in which the ammunition supply worked. The Staff had become so used to unlimited expenditure that batteries were hard pushed to get up and fire the amount ordered.

The 84th B.A.C., under Capt. Constable, had never worked harder or more brilliantly than they did now. All demands from batteries were supplied, although it meant no rest or sleep for Capt. Constable's teams, drivers, officers, or himself.

On 21st October, Le Cateau having now been taken, the battery occupied a position in the shell of a destroyed factory on the outskirts. On 23rd October the battery fired a barrage of 34 lifts in support of our parent-division, the 18th. When the battle started the enemy heavily shelled all around the battery, but the section commanders kept their sections in action, and the battery fulfilled its task. During this advance, when conditions as to food and rest were very primitive, the discipline of the battery was put to a severe test, and stood it without the semblance of a crack.

On 25th October the battery advanced and came into action near Bousies, from which place another attack by the 18th Division was covered. However, on 28th October we were relieved by the 65th Brigade, and withdrew to Le Cateau for a general clear and clean up. But on 3rd November we were again in action near Paul Jacques Farm, and the next day fired a long barrage of 40 lifts in an attack by the 18th Division. This was so successful that on the next day the battery went forward to what was to prove its last fight of the war. A position was chosen in a clearing in the Forêt de Mormal, rather difficult to occupy, but with plenty of material handy. However, the next day, 6th November, the battery withdrew from the chase, marched back to Bousies, and arrived at Maretz on 8th November. Here guns, horses and personnel dug themselves out and prepared for another long trek forward. But already rumours as to an Armistice had reached even the fighting troops, and lo! and behold, almost even before we had quite washed off the grime of two months' hard fighting and continuous trekking, 11 a.m. on 11th November, 1918, was upon us. The last shell had been fired, and all could walk about feeling a certain amount of security and safety from bombs, bullets and crumps.

CHAPTER VIII.

AFTER THE ARMISTICE.

THE battery soon settled down at Maretz, wondering what was going to happen. The joy of winning and chasing the enemy had got into our blood, and we wanted to rout him. And it is hardly to be doubted that we should have had peace signed very much sooner if only the dogs of war had been loose for another week or two. But Foch afterwards said he did not feel justified in risking one more Allied life if he could obtain peace on our terms. And if, instead of the politicians, Foch and Haig had conducted the Peace Conference, probably the seemingly interminable delay would not have occurred. The politicians, having done their utmost, albeit unwittingly, to crab the soldier and lose the war, now had their innings, and failed again miserably. However much we may individually malign the army—and who is there who is not fed up with it at times?—there is no doubt that it does its job, and " gets there."

On the 5th December, 1918, H.M. the King, accompanied by H.R.H. the Prince of Wales, and F.M. Sir Douglas Haig motored through Maretz.

Having been warned of this, we all lined the road, without ceremony, and loudly cheered H.M. The King's car slowed down, and the Royal occupants and the C.-in-C. seemed very pleased with the way we turned out and cheered them.

The time was now taken up in organising race meetings, training our horses (as the owners thought!), and in the making of books. We held a brigade meeting, at which the battery put up some good horses.

On 15th December, 1918, the 18th Division held a race meeting, which attracted large crowds. In the last race of the day Major Grant, who had just ridden a winner, was riding his grey Dolly, and had advised people to back it to win. The mare was nearly blind, and came down at a soft place, losing the race, and very nearly her owner's life also. However, like a bad halfpenny, Major Grant turned up again, from No. 8 General Hospital, Rouen, on 15th January, 1919!

A very happy and joyous Christmas—our fourth in France—was spent at Maretz, although some expected to have had it at their homes, seeing that the Armistice was six weeks' old.

Lieut. H. S. Field, who joined the battery from C/84 in March, 1919, helped us nobly to the end.

On 6th March, 1919, Lt.-Col. Cornes left the brigade, and Major Grant took over the command.

Demobilisation had now begun to take place, although strict orders were received to be ready to take the field at short notice. All ranks, and all horses and mules, were classified and re-classified several times in trades, precedence for demobilisation, retention for Army of Occupation, and heaven knows what else.

On 23rd March, 1919, we moved to the neighbouring village of Bertry, " in order to be near the railhead, Caudry." This raised the hopes of those who wanted to get home very high. But nothing happened, and O.C.'s were at their wits' end to discover ways and means to keep their commands occupied and cheerful. As horses began to go, race meetings were no longer possible. There was a great demand for concert and entertainment parties. The brigade possessed quite a creditable one, and they did their share in keeping everyone in a good humour. Dances were organised, trips to Amiens in motor lorries, hidden treasure hunts, football matches, boxing shows, and an attempt was made to raise enthusiasm for the Army Education Scheme. But what the troops wanted was Blighty. As one song had it :—

> Day after day, and
> Month after month,
> And year after year,
> And still we are here !

However, on 15th April, 1919, the battery came down to its cadre strength of 49. This was afterwards reduced still lower. Eventually all guns and

stores were handed over to the Ordnance Dept.,
and the remnants of a very fine fighting unit came
back to "dear old Blighty," and were formally,
or informally, disbanded at Dover on 17th June,
1919, exactly four years and eight months after its
birth.

AWARDS.

The following awards were won by the under-mentioned officers, N.C.O.'s and men whilst serving in A/84 Bde., R.F.A. :—

Military Cross.

        CAPTAIN E. B. BRASIER-CREAGH
        LIEUT. R. DARLEY
        CAPTAIN A. M. DUFF
        MAJOR D. F. GRANT
        LIEUT. R. K. A. KENNEDY
        LIEUT. R. D. TAYLOR

Military Medal.

        DRIVER J. ACKROYD
        CORPORAL H. ALLUM
        CORPORAL A. F. BETHELL
        GUNNER J. DICKENS
        SERGEANT J. FLEMING
        CORPORAL A. FREEMAN
        DRIVER W. GAGE
        BDR. J. HOOKWAY
        BDR. T. MCMILLAN
        BDR. W. C. MORGAN
        SERGEANT A. J. PORTER
        CORPORAL H. YOUNG

Meritorious Service Medal.

        BDR. H. POOLE

Italian Medal for Military Valour (Bronze).

        BDR. H. POOLE

Mention in Despatches.

        CAPTAIN A. M. DUFF, M.C.
        MAJOR D. F. GRANT, M.C.

THINGS WE SHOULD LIKE TO KNOW.

(AND PERHAPS SOME OF US DO!)

1.—The names of the persons who were affectionately called—

> (a) Old Zepp
> (b) Bathchair-Brighton
> (c) Georgie
> (d) Daddy
> (e) Twisty
> (f) Monkey
> (g) Jock
> (h) Busty
> (i) Flossie
> (j) The Fair-haired Boy
> (k) Mother
> (l) Ginger
> (m) Blue Stockings
> (n) Slops
> (o) Bokki

2.—The qualifications necessary to become a mem-
ber of " G " sub-section.

3.—What happened to the two surplus horses in the
battery on demobilisation.

4.—Why was it that it was usually the iron rations
that were " destroyed by enemy shell fire," and
not those for the day.

5.—Whether it was entirely due to the slippery
state of the road that a certain officer got a
cut on his head at Christmas, 1918.

GLOSSARY OF ABBREVIATIONS.

A.F.G. 1098.	Official name of the inventory, showing the equipment and stores of a battery.
A.D.V.S.	Assistant Director of Veterinary Services.
A.O.D.	Army Ordnance Department.
A.R.P.	Ammunition Refilling Point.
B.A.C.	Brigade Ammunition Column.
B.C.	Battery Commander.
B.G.	Brigadier-General.
B.S.M.	Battery Sergeant Major.
B.Q.M.S.	Battery Quartermaster Sergeant.
C.C.S.	Casualty Clearing Station.
C.R.A.	Commanding Royal Artillery (of a Division).
D.A.D.O.S.	Deputy Assistant Director of Ordnance Supplies.
F.A.T.	Field Artillery Training (the hand-book of training for the R.H. and R.F.A.).
Fokker.	A successful type of German aeroplane.
F.O.O.	Forward Observing Officer. The Artillery Officer who went forward with the first waves of attacking infantry.
G.O.C.	General Officer Commanding.
G.R.O.	General Routine Order, issued by the Commander-in-Chief.
G.S.O.	General Staff Officer.
G.S. wagon.	General Service wagon.
" Hairy."	The nickname for any draught horse.
H.Q.	Head Quarters.
H.V. shell.	High Velocity shell.
I.O.M.	Inspector of Ordnance Machinery.
M.G.	Machine Gun.
O.C.	Officer Commanding.
O.P.	Observation Post, from which Artillery Observers watched the enemy and the effects of our own shooting.
Pop.	Popular abbreviation for the town of Poperinghe.
S.A.A.	Small Arms Ammunition.

INDEX

PAGE.

H.M. the King ... 20, 25, 85
H.R.H. the Prince of
Wales 64, 85

PAGE

Ainchain Farm 77
Allum, Corporal H., M.M. 75
Ammunition Carriers, In-
vention of 42
Ancre, River 25
Argoeuvres 34
Armentieres 40
Armistice ... 84, 85
Authuille Wood (Blighty
Wood) 42, 44

Bazentin Le Grand and
Le Petit 39
Beaurevoir Line 83
Bell, Lt. S. W. W. ... 80
Bertry 87
Bethell, Corporal A. F.,
M.M. 19, 53, 66
Bethune 73, 76
Bewell, R. J., B.Q.M.S.
16, 23
Billon Wood 34
Blois, Lt.-Col. D., D.S.O.
27, 39
Bluett Farm 64
Boom Ravine 46
Boston, Lt. W. T. ... 23
Boussies 84
Bradley, Second Lt. E. ... 74
Brasier - Creagh, Capt.
E. B., M.C. 82

PAGE

Bray sur Somme ... 33
Buire 33
Bury St. Edmunds ... 13
Canadians 41
Carnoy 36
Caterpillar Valley ... 39
Cherry Brandy 78
Cheshire Bde. R.F.A., 2nd 32
Colchester ... 13, 18

Daours 33
Darley, Lt. R., M.C.
23, 37, 62, 69, 75
Delville Wood 40
Dernancourt 25
Dewar, Colonel 17
Dexter, Lt. E. N. 15, 23, 35
Dranoutre 59
Duff, Capt. A. M., M.C. 74

Ecurie 51
Elverdinghe ... 64, 66
English, Col. E., C.M.G.
17, 21, 22, 27
Festubert 73
Field, Lt. H. S. 86
Flash Spotting 65
Fleming, Sgt. J., M.M. 23, 34
Fosse 7 de Bethune ... 79
Frevin Capelle 51
Fricourt 25, 33

PAGE

Gas, Poison ... 33, 39, 74
Grandcourt ... 45, 46
Grand Laviers 43
Grant, Major D. F., M.C.
      15, 74, 82, 86
Griffin, Sec. Lt. H. J. ... 15

Haig, F.M. Sir D. ... 85
Herville 82
Hinchcliffe, Gnr. ... 77
Hindenburg Line ... 83
Holland, Lt.-Gen. Sir T. 79
Holt, Lt. H. B. ... 59, 74
Hookway, Bdr., M.M. 57
Horn, Sec. Lt. F. W. ... 70
Houdain 81
Houleron 77
Houtkerque ... 63, 72

Irles 48

Jones, Sgt. J. J. 23

Kennedy, Lt. R. K. A.,
      M.C. ... 46, 53, 72, 80

La Boiselle 41
Lait, Sec. Lt. C. P. ... 28
Last, Sgt. W. ... 23, 46
Lay, Bdr. W. 54
Le Cateau ... 83, 84
Le Havre ... 24, 76
Le Touret ... 73, 75
Le Vielfort, nr. Bruay 78, 82
Lewer, B.Q.M.S., A. 22, 43
Loos, Battle of 26
" Lucille " 78
Lys Retreat, 1918 ... 75

Maretz 83, 85
Maxse, Lt.-Gen. Sir F. I.,
      K.C.B., C.V.O., D.S.O.
      21, 24, 56
McMillan, Bdr. T.,
      M.M. 37, 54

PAGE

Méaulte 24, 29
Messines, Battle of ... 59
Metcalfe, Brig.-Gen. S. F.,
      C.M.G., D.S.O. 22, 31
Meteor Telegrams 45, 69
Middleton, Sgt. 23
Mormal, Forêt de ... 84

Nab Junction 45
Nutter, Gnr. W. ... 74
Observation Post
      27, 36, 58, 69, 72
Olney, Tptr. A. P. 20, 37, 45
Oppy 53, 55

Paschendaele 64
Paterson, Capt. A.,
      D.S.O., M.C. ... 43, 45, 51
Phillips, Sec. Lt. J. P. ... 28
Pickwick, Bdr. A. J. ... 71
Pilkem 66
Platts, Lt. J. E. A. 35, 51, 53
Plumer, F.M., Lord ... 60
Poperinghe 63
Porter, Sgt. A. J., M.M. 57
Portuguese Army ... 75
Pozieres 42

Rawlinson, Gen. Lord ... 36
Reorganisation of Bat-
      tery 43, 50
Riach, Driver C. ... 51
Rice, Capt. F. J., M.C.
      15, 22, 23, 25, 43
Ridout, B.Q.M.S., E. 43, 79
Roclincourt 52
Rubrouck 72

St. Julien 68
St. Momelin 67
St. Venant 77
Salisbury Plain 18
Schofield, Lt. F. P. 33, 48
Schwaben Redoubt ... 42

PAGE

Seagram, Brig.-Gen.
  T. O., D.S.O. 22
Shaw, Sgt. T. A.   ... 23
Shrapnel Corner   ... 62
Somme, Battle of   36, 46
Southwick, Corp. A.   ... 60
Spot Farm   69
Steenbeek   ...   67, 68
Steptoe, Bdr. J. C. 27, 33, 54
Stone, Brig.-Gen. F. G.,
  C.M.G.   ...   21, 27
Straubenzee, Maj.-Gen.
  C. van, C.B. ...   22, 27
Stuff Redoubt   42
Suzanne 33

"T" Battery, R.H.A. ... 33
Tanks   42
Taylor, Lt. R. D., M.C.   78
Taylor, Capt. W., M.C. 43, 51

PAGE

" Tests "   30
Thiepval 41
Trois Rois   ...   62, 63
Turner, B.S.M., F. H.,
  D.C.M.   ... 19, 23, 79

Venneear, Corp. R.   14, 43
Vermelles   81
Ville sur Ancre ...   25, 29
Vimy Ridge, Battle of ... 51
Vincent, Farrier Sgt. ... 23

Ward, Sec. Lt. R.   ... 74
Warren Heath, Ipswich 16
Wetten, Fitter   53
Wieltje 68
Willerval   55

Zillebeke Lake 61

LIST OF OFFICERS who served in "A" BATTERY, 84th BRIGADE, R.F.A.

NAME.	PERIOD.	RANK IN A/84.	NATURE OF CASUALTY ON LEAVING.
Allen, S.	April, 1916.	Lieut.	Posted B/84 Brigade R.F.A.
Allen, W. G.	April—May, 1916.	Lieut.	Posted 18 Division Trench Mortars.
Bagshaw, E. L.	March—April, 1918.	Lieut.	Hospital, sick.
Bell, S. W. W.	October, 1917—May, 1919.	Lieut.	Posted as O.C. Fire Defence, Dieppe.
Boston, W. T.	17th October, 1914—July, 1915.	Lieut.	Posted 84th B.A.C.
Bradley, E.	February—March, 1918.	2nd Lieut.	Wounded 22nd March, 1918.
Brasier-Creagh, E. B., M.C.	September, 1918—March, 1919.	Capt.	Posted D/84.
Clutterbuck, G. W. ...	September, 1917.	Lieut.	Wounded 29th September, 1917.
Darley, R... M.C. ...	January, 1915—April, 1918.	Lieut.	Wounded 14th April, 1918.
Dean, C. W.	July—August, 1917.	Lieut.	Re-posted 84th B.A.C.
Dexter, E. N.	17th October, 1914—June, 1916.	Lieut.	Home, sick, June 1916.
Duff, A. M., M.C. ...	February—July, 1918.	Capt.	Home.
Field, H. S.	March—June, 1919.	Lieut.	Demobilised 27th June, 1919.
Gardiner, L. B.	May—September, 1917.	Lieut.	Posted H.Q. 84th Brigade, R.F.A.
Gibbon, F. S.	February—March, 1916.	Lieut.	Accidentally injured, March, 1916.
Grant, D. F., M.C. ...	17th October, 1914—May, 1919.	Major	Posted Army of Rhine, 26th May, 1919.
Griffin, H. J.	17th October—December, 1914.	2nd Lieut.	Posted D/84 Brigade, R.F.A.
Holt, B. B.	{ January—March, 1917, & { July, 1917—April, 1919.	Lieut.	{ Wounded March, 1917. { Posted Army of Rhine, April, 1919.
Horn, F. W.	November, 1917.	2nd Lieut.	Wounded, November, 1917.
Kennedy, R. K. A., M.C. ...	{ January, 1917—March, 1918, & { June, 1918—February, 1919.	Lieut.	{ Posted R.H.A., March, 1918. { Demobilised, February, 1919.
Lait, C. P.	January—February, 1916.	Lieut.	Posted D/84 Brigade, R.F.A.
Leslie-Stuart, S. ...	January—February, 1918.	Capt.	Re-posted H.Q. 84th Brigade, R.F.A.
Morris, T. H.	June, 1918.	2nd Lieut.	Posted 56 D.A.C.
Paterson, A. A. A., D.S.O., M.C.	December, 1916—February, 1917.	Capt.	Posted as O.C. C/83 Brigade, R.F.A.
Phillips, J. P.	January, 1916.	Lieut.	Posted 84 B.A.C.
Platts, J. E. A.	June, 1916—April, 1917.	Lieut.	Wounded 9th April, 1917.
Rainsford, H. B. ...	July, 1918.	2nd Lieut.	Posted Base.
Rice, F. J., M.C. ...	17th Oct., 1914—Dec., 1916.	2nd Lieut.	Posted Capt. of C/82 Brigade R.F.A.
Saunders	October, 1914.	Lieut.	Posted R.F.C.
Schofield, F. P. ...	March, 1916—August, 1917.	Lieut.	Home, August, 1917.
Taylor, R. D., M.C. ...	November, 1917—April, 1919.	Capt.	Posted Army of Rhine.
Taylor, W., M.C. ...	December, 1916—February, 1918.	2nd Lieut.	Posted 4th Army Artillery School.
Ward, J. H.	March, 1918.	Lieut.	Wounded, 22nd March, 1918.
Whitfield, E.	June, 1918—April, 1919.	Lieut.	Posted Army of Rhine.
Wise, M. A.	June—July, 1918.	Lieut.	Posted B/84 Brigade, R.F.A.

Printed in Great Britain by
Amazon.co.uk, Ltd.,
Marston Gate.